100 Ideas for Primary Teachers:
RSE

Catherine Kirk

BLOOMSBURY EDUCATION
LONDON OXFORD NEW YORK NEW DELHI SYDNEY

BLOOMSBURY EDUCATION
Bloomsbury Publishing Plc
50 Bedford Square, London, WC1B 3DP, UK
29 Earlsfort Terrace, Dublin 2, Ireland

BLOOMSBURY, BLOOMSBURY EDUCATION and the Diana logo are trademarks of Bloomsbury Publishing Plc

First published in Great Britain, 2025 by Bloomsbury Publishing Plc
This edition published in Great Britain, 2025 by Bloomsbury Publishing Plc

Text copyright © Catherine Kirk, 2025

Catherine Kirk has asserted her right under the Copyright, Designs and Patents Act, 1988, to be identified as Author of this work

Bloomsbury Publishing Plc does not have any control over, or responsibility for, any third-party websites referred to or in this book. All internet addresses given in this book were correct at the time of going to press. The author and publisher regret any inconvenience caused if addresses have changed or sites have ceased to exist, but can accept no responsibility for any such changes

All rights reserved. No part of this publication may be reproduced or transmitted in any form or by any means, electronic or mechanical, including photocopying, recording, or any information storage or retrieval system, without prior permission in writing from the publishers

A catalogue record for this book is available from the British Library

ISBN: PB: 978-1-8019-9448-4; ePDF: 978-1-8019-9447-7; ePub: 978-1-8019-9450-7

2 4 6 8 10 9 7 5 3 1

Typeset by Newgen KnowledgeWorks Pvt. Ltd., Chennai, India
Printed and bound in in the UK by CPI Group Ltd, CR0 4YY

MIX
Paper | Supporting responsible forestry
FSC® C013604

To find out more about our authors and books visit www.bloomsbury.com and sign up for our newsletters

Contents

Acknowledgements	vi
Introduction	vii
How to use this book	viii

Part 1: Background — **1**
- 1 What is RSE? — 2
- 2 Legislation — 3
- 3 Evidence base — 4
- 4 Key organisations — 5
- 5 Pedagogy — 6
- 6 Safeguarding — 7
- 7 How RSE fits with broader PSHE — 8

Part 2: Intent, implementation and impact — **9**
- 8 Vision, values and ethos — 10
- 9 Pupil voice — 11
- 10 Consultation — 12
- 11 To scheme or not to scheme — 14
- 12 Using data — 16
- 13 Transition — 17
- 14 What makes an effective RSE lesson? — 18
- 15 Cross-curricular — 19
- 16 External providers — 20
- 17 Measuring impact — 21
- 18 Learning walks — 22

Part 3: Parents — **23**
- 19 Parent engagement — 24
- 20 Open-talk café — 25
- 21 Homework and projects — 26
- 22 Parent meetings — 27
- 23 Parent workshop — 28
- 24 Parent advisory group — 30
- 25 Website — 31

Part 4: Creating a safe learning environment — **33**
- 26 Keeping children safe — 34
- 27 Group agreement — 36

28 Supporting children to access help	38
29 Managing disclosures	40
30 SEND	41
31 Equality and protected characteristics	42
32 LGBT	44
33 Faith	46

Part 5: Preparing to teach — **47**
34 Assessing training needs	48
35 Unconscious bias	50
36 Values	52
37 CPD	53
38 Networking	54
39 Support	55
40 Improving knowledge	56
41 Key messages	58

Part 6: Being creative with RSE delivery — **59**
42 Participatory RSE	60
43 Drama techniques	61
44 Continuum	62
45 Scenarios	64
46 Stories	66
47 Conscience Alley	67
48 Mood boards	68
49 Props	69
50 Sculpture	70
51 Puppets	71
52 Crafts	72
53 Pupil action	73

Part 7: Gender, bodies and safety — **75**
54 Language and terminology	76
55 Naming genitals	77
56 Body safety and consent	78
57 Breaking stereotype boxes	79
58 Personal space	80
59 Female genital mutilation (FGM)	82
60 Transgender	84

Part 8: Healthy relationships — **85**
61 Friendship gardens	86
62 Family drawing relay	88
63 Qualities of healthy friendships	89
64 Quotes	90
65 Anti-bullying photo exhibition	91

66	Emotional dominoes	92
67	Wedding speeches	94
68	Relationship snapshots	95
69	Safety detectives	96

Part 9: Puberty — **99**

70	What to teach and when	100
71	Continuum of normal	101
72	Anatomy	102
73	Puberty comic strips	104
74	Puberty bag	106
75	Problem texts	108
76	Adverts	109
77	Puberty bingo	110
78	Menstruation	112
79	Masturbation	113

Part 10: Sex — **115**

80	Making the choice to start a family	116
81	Family identity boxes	117
82	Reproduction	118
83	Sensory stations	120
84	Sexual consent	122
85	Contraception	124
86	Parenting	125

Part 11: Questions and challenging issues — **127**

87	Questions, questions, questions	128
88	Question box	130
89	Personal questions	131
90	Explicit questions	132
91	Encouraging questions	133
92	Scripting	134

Part 12: Assessment and evidence — **135**

93	What and why?	136
94	Draw and Write	137
95	Brainstorm	138
96	Role-play	139
97	Floorbooks	140
98	Quizzes	141
99	RAG-rating	142
100	Displays, podcasts, leaflets	143

References — 144

Acknowledgements

Firstly, I would like to thank the many teachers with whom I have worked over the years. Your dedication, passion and creativity inspire me.

Thank you to all the children I have had the privilege of teaching. You have taught me as much as I have taught you. Thanks for your questions, your insights and for making each lesson a rewarding experience.

To the amazing colleagues with whom I have worked throughout my career: your support and encouragement have been invaluable. Thank you for pushing me to improve, innovate and have confidence in my abilities. Special thanks to Amanda, Andy, Cathy, Chris, Claire, Clare, DJ, Jane, Jasmin, John, Josie, Karen, Linda, Marie, Mark, Martin, Megan, Pat, Phil, Polly, Randall, Rebecca and Sue. Thanks to Ian and Ester for giving feedback on the draft; I appreciate your support.

Mark and Tobias, thank you for your love, belief and understanding. Your patience and encouragement have allowed me to pursue my passions and dedicate the time needed to create this book. I love you both so much.

To my friends and family, thanks for being there for me, cheering me on and cheering me up! Helene, Jane, Hazel, Jodie and Susan – without you to put the world to rights with, where would I be?

Finally, I would like to acknowledge the broader RSE community, including researchers, policymakers and advocates who tirelessly work to improve and champion RSE for all children. Your efforts are making a significant difference in the lives of children everywhere.

Thank you all for being part of this journey. This book is a testament to our shared commitment to providing high-quality RSE to children, empowering them with the knowledge and skills that they need to navigate the world with confidence and respect.

Catherine Kirk

Introduction

Welcome to *100 Ideas for Primary Teachers: RSE*. As an experienced relationships and sex education (RSE) practitioner, I have spent over 20 years working with children and teachers to develop and deliver effective, engaging and age-appropriate RSE. This book brings together my experiences and insights and is designed to support educators to develop their practice and create meaningful and impactful RSE.

RSE is a vital part of a child's education. It empowers children to develop respectful relationships, understand their bodies and make informed choices. With the rise of digital communication and social media, it is more important than ever for children to have a solid foundation in RSE to navigate the complexities of modern life.

Throughout my career, I have seen first hand the positive impact that effective RSE can have on children. It helps them to build empathy, develop self-awareness and gain the confidence to express their thoughts and feelings. These skills are not only essential for their personal wellbeing but also lay the groundwork for future relationships.

This book is structured to cover key aspects of RSE, including practical advice on creating a positive RSE environment, handling sensitive questions, and involving parents and carers. These tips are based on my years of experience and are designed to help you to navigate the challenges that can arise when teaching RSE. There are also many RSE teaching and activity ideas to try out with your children.

There are a range of terms to describe education around relationships, sex and health education. Whilst I have used the English terms, RSE and Personal, Social and Health Education (PSHE), the ideas in this book can be applied in schools across the four nations of the UK.

100 Ideas for Primary Teachers: RSE is a toolkit designed to empower you to deliver effective, safe and engaging RSE. By integrating these ideas into your planning and teaching of RSE, you will help children to build the skills and knowledge that they need to thrive, both in and out of the classroom. I hope that this book is a source of inspiration to review and revitalise your RSE delivery. Together, we can ensure that every child receives the comprehensive, thoughtful and supportive RSE that they deserve.

How to use this book

This book includes simple, practical and tried-and-tested ideas to enhance your RSE provision.

Each idea includes:

- a catchy title, easy to refer to and share with your colleagues
- an interesting quote linked to the idea
- a summary of the idea in bold, making it easy to flick through the book and identify an idea you want to use at a glance
- a step-by-step guide to implementing the idea.

Each idea also includes one or more of the following:

Teaching tip
Practical tips and advice for how and how not to run the activity or put the idea into practice.

Taking it further
Ideas and advice for how to extend the idea or develop it further.

Bonus idea ★
There are 31 bonus ideas in this book that are extra-exciting, extra-original and extra-interesting.

Share how you use these ideas and find out what other practitioners have done using **#100Ideas**.

Background

Part 1

IDEA 1

What is RSE?

'Is it the Year 6 sex talk?'

Primary relationships and sex education (RSE) provides children with age-appropriate information about relationships, body safety, puberty and sex. Tailored to the developmental stage of children, it aims to equip them with the knowledge, skills and understanding necessary to have healthy relationships, make informed choices and keep safe.

Teaching tip

A comprehensive RSE curriculum empowers children to make informed decisions as they grow older. It promotes healthy attitudes, allows children the opportunity to explore risks and consequences, and fosters a supportive environment where children feel comfortable seeking guidance when needed.

Taking it further

Keep up to date with RSE by following relevant organisations, such as the Sex Education Forum, on social media channels.

Historically, RSE has had its fair share of controversy, usually where parts of the content have been taken out of context or sensationalised by the media. In reality, children learn knowledge and skills at relevant ages to promote informed and healthy decision-making.

In effective primary RSE, through a spiral curriculum, children are taught about:

- anatomy, including naming genitals, and the understanding of privacy, personal space, consent, and safe touch
- healthy relationships, both on- and offline, including friendships, families, boundaries, communication, unhealthy behaviours and conflict resolution
- the physical and emotional changes of puberty and how to manage them
- sex, consent, reproduction, pregnancy and birth
- respect for differences and challenging stereotypes.

IDEA 2

Legislation

'Legislation guides RSE delivery in schools.'

Government guidance around RSE varies from nation to nation across the UK.

Over recent years, RSE in the UK has undergone significant legislative changes aimed at modernising the curriculum and supporting the diverse needs of children. Legislation reflects societal shifts, acknowledging the importance of a comprehensive approach to RSE that reinforces healthy relationships, consent, body autonomy and internet safety.

Modern legislative frameworks emphasise the need for RSE to be inclusive, ensuring that all children, regardless of their background, needs or identity, receive RSE that is relevant. This inclusivity fosters an environment where children feel safe, seen and respected.

Legislation across the nations focuses on the importance of putting healthy relationships at the forefront of RSE, equipping children with the knowledge and skills to form and maintain these while recognising behaviours that are not healthy.

The legislative framework, along with evidence-based practice, should be the starting point for developing comprehensive RSE. Keep abreast of legislative changes by joining local or national RSE networks and signing up to mailing lists of RSE organisations.

Teaching tip

Check out the framework or guidance for RSE that covers your setting.

IDEA 3

Evidence base

'You're taking away their innocence.'

Despite concerns often targeted at RSE, evidence tells us that comprehensive RSE does not lead to earlier sexual activity, and instead has protective effects.

There is a clear evidence base for the effectiveness of comprehensive RSE. In primary RSE, we are supporting children to make healthy, informed choices about their current and future relationships, and are laying the foundations for more in-depth education in later years around sex and sexual health. Our key aim is also to keep children safe from harm.

- An evidence review by UNESCO in 2009 found that curriculum-based RSE programmes do not have harmful effects and do not hasten the initiation of sexual activity or increase sexual activity.
- In the 2015 document 'Personal, social, health and economic education: A review of impact and effective practice', the government outlines the evidence base for effective RSE. They note that RSE has been shown to 'reduce unwanted pregnancies' and 'increase the likelihood of pupils using contraception' when they do have sex (DfE, 2015, p. 5).
- The Sex Education Forum (2022) quotes evidence from a Cochrane review in 2015, which found that 'children who are taught about preventing sexual abuse at schools are more likely to tell an adult if they had or were experiencing sexual abuse' (p. 6). They also quote Goldfarb and Lieberman's 2021 review, which concludes that one of the most common consequences of sex abuse curricula in the US and Canada is 'increased knowledge of a resource person to whom children would report abuse' (p. 6).

Teaching tip

The NSPCC (2023) found that the RSE children receive is still patchy and often poor. Young people want teachers to listen to them about what they would like to learn. They want to be involved in building a creative learning environment and want providers of RSE to be comfortable and confident.

Taking it further

Engaging with relevant organisations in your nation will help you to keep up to date.

IDEA 4

Key organisations

'There are loads of online forums and it's sometimes difficult to know where to get the most accurate information.'

Linking with key organisations supports good-quality RSE and helps you to keep up to date with recent developments.

There are many organisations that provide support to schools with RSE and related issues:

- **PSHE Association:** The professional body for PSHE, offering guidance, curriculum frameworks, lesson plans and training. There are some free materials plus paid membership options.
- **Sex Education Forum:** A charity that campaigns for effective RSE. It offers evidence briefings, guidance and training. There are some free materials plus paid membership options.
- **NSPCC:** Resources and advice for parents and professionals on keeping children safe. There are resources for RSE, including the free 'Let's Talk Pants' materials to teach about body autonomy and consent.
- **Anti-bullying Alliance:** Information and tools for anti-bullying work. They lead on the annual Anti-Bullying Week in November.
- **Childnet**: A charity providing guidance and resources for children, parents and professionals on how to keep safe online.

Your local authority education or public health teams may also offer support with PSHE or healthy schools and can signpost to useful resources and training. They may also run networks, which are a great place to share practice with other schools in your local area.

> **Teaching tip**
>
> Sign up to the mailing lists of key organisations to ensure that you are notified when new information is released.

IDEA 5

Pedagogy

'It requires a slightly different approach to other subjects; it's more about exploration and discussion, not just giving information.'

RSE has its own pedagogy: an interactive and holistic approach that supports critical thinking and the development of knowledge and skills.

Some characteristics of RSE pedagogy:

- The content of RSE should be tailored to be appropriate and relevant for the age and stage of development of the children. It should be subject to regular reflection and review.
- RSE is inclusive; it is delivered in a non-judgemental manner, including diverse backgrounds, cultures and identities.
- RSE is planned in a holistic way, covering biological, emotional, social and ethical dimensions. There is an emphasis on the importance of healthy relationships, consent, communication skills and emotional wellbeing.
- RSE delivery is interactive and participatory, to encourage thinking, discussion and questions. Lessons involve group activities, role-play, scenarios and case studies, and lots of opportunity for questions.
- RSE supports critical thinking skills, encouraging children to question stereotypes, challenge myths and analyse the impact of the media.
- RSE promotes the development of knowledge and skills and explores values and beliefs.
- Through RSE, children apply their learning to real life through case studies and scenarios.
- RSE is delivered in partnership with parents and carers; they have a key role to play in supporting children's learning.
- RSE should be delivered safely with signposting to support.

> **Bonus idea** ★
>
> Providing access to effective professional development opportunities and current research, good practice-sharing and networking will help those teaching RSE to feel skilled and confident to do so.

IDEA 6

Safeguarding

'As a safeguarding lead, RSE is vital for teaching children the knowledge and skills to navigate risk, recognise abusive behaviours and seek help and support.'

RSE is the key delivery vehicle for teaching preventative education that supports safeguarding. There need to be close links between the designated safeguarding lead (DSL) and those planning and delivering RSE, to ensure that opportunities for keeping children safe are maximised.

RSE should be both proactive and reactive to current issues within the school. It is good practice for the DSL and RSE lead to meet regularly and/or have processes in place for sharing relevant information.

The RSE curriculum should allow flexibility to enable emerging issues to be explored; for example, if the DSL learns that children are sharing inappropriate content online, the RSE lead can review what is currently in the curriculum to teach about risks and online safety, and whether this needs strengthening. This should not be a knee-jerk reaction, but rather a considered approach to developing the RSE curriculum to meet needs.

Similarly, it is useful for the DSL to know what is being delivered in RSE in case particular lessons trigger disclosures of a safeguarding nature – for example, a lesson on unhealthy relationships or safe/unsafe touch.

Children should be signposted to support in each lesson, both within and outside of school (see Idea 28), and lessons should be delivered safely with appropriate boundaries (see Idea 26).

Teaching tip

Be mindful of children's body language in RSE sessions, particularly those covering more sensitive topics. Record any unusual reactions or behaviour using your school's reporting system.

IDEA 7

How RSE fits with broader PSHE

'There is so much cross over between RSE and PSHE, we really need to make connections for the children.'

RSE should be delivered as part of a broader comprehensive programme of personal, social, health and economic (PSHE) education; it is not a standalone subject.

> **Teaching tip**
>
> When delivering PSHE, look for opportunities to highlight links to RSE learning for the children.

PSHE covers a wide range of topics related to health, wellbeing, safety, personal development and financial literacy. RSE is a component within PSHE, with a narrower focus on topics such as relationships, body awareness, puberty, sex and reproduction. While RSE tends to address specific aspects within the wider PSHE curriculum, both are interconnected and integral to a comprehensive educational approach.

In the past, RSE was often taught as a block of lessons at a particular point in the year, primarily focusing on puberty and sex education without adequately exploring relationships. A more holistic approach intertwines RSE with broader PSHE themes, recognising the interdependence between healthy relationships, personal development and overall wellbeing.

Effective integration of RSE into PSHE involves drawing connections between specific RSE content and broader PSHE topics. For example, in a lesson on emotions and mental health in PSHE, children can explore the significance of relationships in supporting positive mental wellbeing.

This integrated approach to RSE and PSHE not only broadens children's perspectives but also equips them with practical skills and knowledge to navigate various life situations.

Part 2

Intent, implementation and impact

IDEA 8

Vision, values and ethos

'Everyone understands what we are working towards in RSE.'

Your school's vision, values and ethos should guide your provision of RSE and PSHE. Developing an RSE charter ensures that all stakeholders are clear about your aims.

Teaching tip

Refer to the charter when delivering lessons.

In partnership with parents, staff and pupils, develop a charter that outlines your vision and values for RSE. Start the process with a brainstorming session with key representatives from each stakeholder group. At this meeting, brainstorm what you want to achieve through your provision of RSE, using these questions as a guide:

- What is the vision for RSE?
- What are you trying to achieve?
- What values do you want to promote?
- What key messages do you want to give?
- How does RSE reflect core school values?

Develop a draft charter based on the brainstorming session. Circulate this to stakeholders for consultation. Produce a final version based on feedback, create posters to display in school and add to the website. Here are some sample statements for an RSE charter.

At this school, our provision of RSE:

- is based on the needs of our children
- aims to keep our children safe
- reflects our school values of respect, resilience and kindness
- promotes healthy relationships
- is delivered in partnership with parents
- is inclusive of all children and families
- is delivered in a non-judgemental, unbiased, honest manner
- gives the children the information they need
- develops children's skills to make healthy, informed choices.

Bonus idea ★

Developing a charter can be particularly useful where there are parental concerns about RSE. This transparent process allows parents to appreciate the overall vision for RSE and what the school is trying to achieve.

IDEA 9

Pupil voice

'Pupils are the most insightful critics of your RSE programme.'

RSE should meet the needs of pupils. Regular pupil voice can inform the planning and monitoring of RSE.

Pupil voice can shape the RSE curriculum, influencing what topics are covered, how RSE is taught and the resources used. If you have a school council, pupils could be given a specific task to gather the views of their classmates on RSE and report back. Other methods include surveys, exit slips after lessons or an RSE suggestions box in the school. Here are some sample questions for pupil voice:

- What do you like about RSE?
- Are there any bits that you don't like?
- What do you remember from RSE lessons?
- What would make RSE better?
- What questions do you have about... ?
- How do you feel in RSE lessons?
- What would make you feel better?
- How safe do you feel in RSE lessons?
- How included do you feel in RSE lessons?
- What would make lessons more interesting?
- What is a healthy friendship?
- How can we can talk about these things in a way everyone can understand?
- What are the most important things for children of your age to learn?
- Is there anything that you wished you'd learned earlier?
- Who can help children?

Pupil voice activities not only benefit you as a teacher or RSE lead, but also signal to children that they have agency within the school and that their opinions matter. By expressing their views, children are nurturing their skills of reflection and analysis.

Teaching tip

Try not to guide the children; ask open questions. Be clear on the outcomes of the discussion, e.g. not all their views will be acted upon, as they may contradict.

IDEA 10

Consultation

'It was pleasing to see how much support there is for RSE from parents.'

When reviewing your RSE policy and curriculum, it is good practice to consult with your parents and carers to ensure that their views are considered.

> **Teaching tip**
>
> Clearly define boundaries when consulting on your RSE policy. Ensure flexibility for changes but remind parents they cannot veto content. Follow the majority while considering minority views.

In some nations of the UK, it is a legal requirement to carry out a parental consultation when reviewing your RSE policy and curriculum. Even where no legislative requirement exists, a consultation offers some valuable benefits to your school's provision of RSE:

- It increases parental involvement.
- It demonstrates respect for different beliefs.
- It enables you to tailor the curriculum – parents know their children best and can give useful insights into what they feel is important.
- It shows transparency and builds trust.
- It addresses any concerns that parents may have.
- It increases your awareness of parents who have knowledge and skills to support your RSE provision, e.g. healthcare professionals.
- It reduces the stigma of RSE.

A useful approach for carrying out the policy consultation is given below:

- Put the draft policy and curriculum on your website (offer translations if relevant, to ensure accessibility).
- Circulate a virtual or paper survey to parents.
- Analyse the results.
- Present findings and proposed amendments at a meeting (see Idea 22) and share via email.
- Share the final policy.

Here are some sample survey questions (choose those that are most relevant for your nation and context):

- Are you aware of the requirements of statutory RSE?
- Do you understand the approach that we are taking to RSE?
- Do you have enough information on how RSE fits in with our school ethos and values?
- Are you aware of how RSE will be taught across the school?
- Do you understand what will be taught in each year group?
- Do you have enough information about what your child(ren) will be learning?
- Is our RSE policy clear?
- Would you like the opportunity to view the resources to be used in RSE? If yes, are there any topics that are of particular interest?
- Would you be interested in attending a workshop to explore how to talk with your child about RSE topics?
- Do you understand the elements of RSE from which parents can withdraw their child and the process for doing so?
- Do you have any further questions or comments on our RSE provision?
- Would you like to be involved in our parent working group for RSE?

Working together with parents can lead to workable solutions to any contentious areas raised through the consultation.

Taking it further

In addition to your parental consultation, provide opportunities for other stakeholders to share their views through surveys, focus groups, staff meetings, governor meetings and pupil voice (see Idea 9). The policy and curriculum should be informed by the needs and views of all.

IDEA 11

To scheme or not to scheme

'RSE should meet the needs of the children within each setting.'

There are many schemes available to teach PSHE, including RSE, and the market continues to grow. A scheme offers some security for both the PSHE lead and the staff delivering it; however, it may limit creativity and flexibility.

While some schools choose to use a curriculum framework provided by their local authority, trust or the PSHE Association to plan and deliver their PSHE/RSE, others will opt for a scheme. Outlined below are some of the pros and cons of using a scheme.

Teaching tip

While feedback on schemes in online forums may be useful, choices about a scheme should be made based on the needs of the children within your school.

Pros

- There is a consistency; you know what everyone is teaching and this can be shared with parents and other interested parties.
- A scheme can build confidence for staff who are anxious about teaching specific parts of RSE or are less experienced.
- Schemes often come with assessment tools.
- Some companies offer other benefits, such as additional topical lessons and training.
- Many schemes will have progression built in.

Cons

- Staff may become over-reliant on the scheme and not develop confidence in creating their own content.
- Schemes are not written with your children/community in mind and therefore may not meet their specific needs.
- The lessons are often formulaic, which may become boring and predictable for children and staff.
- There may be an over-reliance on PowerPoint slides and worksheets, rather than more active learning.

- Schemes can be expensive and may have an annual subscription fee.
- They may not be updated regularly.

Tips for choosing and using a scheme

- Ask staff what they want and need from a scheme – for example, do they want videos included, resources to photocopy or assessment?
- Ask for samples or a 'test-drive' before purchasing.
- Ensure that materials can be shared with parents.
- Check compliance with the RSE requirements for your nation.
- Encourage staff to be creative, whether using a scheme or not.
- Adapt the scheme to meet the needs of your children; change or add to content to ensure relevance.
- Remember the scheme is a vehicle for the delivery of your planned RSE. Be clear with parents about your aims for RSE and how the scheme helps to deliver these rather than allowing the scheme to lead your provision.

If you choose to use a particular scheme, ensure that feedback is sought from pupils and staff on an annual basis to monitor the effectiveness. Do not be afraid to change the scheme if it is not meeting your outcomes.

> **Bonus idea** ★
>
> If using a scheme, set up a shared drive where staff can upload ideas and resources that they have used, to supplement the scheme.

IDEA 12

Using data

'Because the prevalence of domestic abuse in our area is so high, we added additional content to give pupils the opportunity to explore in more depth.'

Data helps schools to plan RSE that meets the needs of pupils. There should be ongoing flexibility to ensure that the curriculum is right for your pupils.

Teaching tip

Engage in local professional development opportunities to keep abreast of current trends.

Taking it further

In a school with a high faith population, you could include more specific references to faith perspectives, in addition to covering relevant laws about relationships. In an area with high teenage pregnancy rates, you may decide to introduce some basic input on contraception in Year 6, as well as strengthening learning around consent and the responsibilities of parenting.

Bonus idea ★

Ask teachers to keep a note of any questions asked by pupils that go beyond the taught content.

To create a programme that meets pupil needs, use relevant data to inform how you deliver RSE. Some sources of data that may be useful in planning your programme include:

- **Demographic:** Look at who is in your school and community to highlight areas of need.
- **Local data and trends:** The Public Health Fingertips site gives information about health in geographical areas.
- **Teachers:** Gather feedback on RSE from teachers delivering the curriculum.
- **Pupil voice:** Learn from the views of your pupils. See Idea 9 for more information on how to gather pupil voice.
- **Parents:** Parents may share useful data, such as current trends on social media, things that are concerning their child or questions that they are being asked about RSE issues.
- **Pupil health behaviour surveys:** Some local authorities run health behaviour surveys for pupils that give an insight into current trends.
- **Incident reports:** Consider the prevalance of particular incidents in schools, for example bullying or use of homophobic language.
- **Assessment data:** This gives you an idea of whether children are achieving the outcomes set and whether more or less challenging content is needed.
- **Pastoral support and safeguarding:** Explore emerging trends for children accessing pastoral support or being flagged by the DSL.

IDEA 13

Transition

'The guide helped me to gain an understanding of how our programme builds on what has been taught before.'

RSE in the primary school should lay the foundations for later learning. Below are some steps for supporting smooth transition to secondary RSE through an RSE transition guide.

The variance in approaches to RSE in primary can mean that secondary colleagues are faced with a daunting task when planning their curriculum for new pupils. An RSE transition guide gives you the opportunity to share key information with your local secondary schools. This will aid in the progression of the children's learning in RSE by providing insights into topics and concepts already covered.

Here are some examples of what could be included:

- the aims and ethos of your RSE provision
- a brief overview of the topics covered in each year group
- the teaching methods used
- what has been covered in the year leading up to transition
- what elements of puberty and sex education have been delivered
- recommended topics to revisit
- a summary of parent engagement
- feedback from pupils about what they enjoy about RSE.

Teaching tip

Share the quick guide with parents and governors to give an insight into your RSE programme.

IDEA 14

What makes an effective RSE lesson?

'All children were really engaged and doing great thinking.'

An effective RSE lesson is one that meets the needs of the children, where everyone feels safe and able to contribute.

Teaching tip

Get into the habit of reflecting on and refining your RSE teaching by RAG-rating the elements listed in this idea after each lesson.

Taking it further

To ensure RSE lessons are truly effective, encourage pupils to apply the learning to real-life situations, through scenarios and examples. Give them the opportunity to reflect on their learning.

What would we see in an effective RSE lesson?

- The content is age- and stage-appropriate for the children and reflects the school's values and ethos.
- There are clear outcomes.
- There is a focus on skills development, exploring attitudes and values.
- The lesson is delivered in a non-judgemental and unbiased way.
- Information given is accurate and up to date.
- The lesson is placed within the context of the topic and/or scheme.
- A group agreement (see Idea 27) is in place and is a working document that is referred to during the lesson.
- Children feel safe and supported and engage with one another in a respectful manner.
- All children are engaged and contribute.
- All children can access the lesson in a way that meets their individual needs.
- A range of interactive teaching methods are used.
- Assessment methods are used to evidence progress.
- Children have opportunities to discuss and ask questions.
- The content and resources used reflect the diversity of the school and broader society.
- Children can articulate what they are learning.
- Children are signposted to appropriate sources of support, in and out of school.

IDEA 15

Cross-curricular

'We can make strong connections for children by covering RSE learning in other subject areas.'

You can maximise the effectiveness of RSE by supplementing stand alone lessons with cross-curricular learning opportunities.

Finding time for comprehensive RSE is often difficult when there is already so much to cover in the primary curriculum. By building on key concepts through other curriculum areas, you help children to retain knowledge and understanding, develop skills and confidence, and explore their own and others' attitudes and values. Here are some examples of where RSE can be supplemented by a cross-curricular approach:

- **Religious education:** Focus on common relationship values shared by many faiths – for example, kindness, respect and empathy.
- **History:** When exploring the war and evacuees, focus on the feelings of loss that children would have experienced, and the skills that they used to build new relationships.
- **Physical education:** Teach the importance of personal hygiene when exercising to reinforce messages given in puberty education.
- **Maths:** Create simple family budgets to explore the responsibilities of parenting.
- **Science:** Explore growth and development in plants, animals and humans.
- **Literacy:** Highlight relationship qualities when reading fiction books.
- **Geography:** Focus on cultural differences between families in different places.

Teaching tip

Articulate the links for your children so that they can relate learning back to RSE: 'The evacuees in our story are feeling loss. Can you remember when we covered this in our RSE lesson? What did we learn?'

Taking it further

Formalise these cross-curricular opportunities in your curriculum plan for RSE.

IDEA 16

External providers

'I was impressed by the depth of knowledge of the facilitator and the careful handling of questions.'

An external provider can add value to your RSE provision. Given the sensitivity of the subject, careful consideration should be given to selecting the right provider.

Bringing in a visitor to support your RSE delivery can add value in a number of ways: novelty and engagement from children; a unique opportunity for you to observe the children as they interact with the visitor; specialist knowledge, expertise and resources; objectivity and unbiased delivery; up-to-date information; and professional development for teachers.

Your local authority or trust may be able to signpost you to visitors on particular RSE themes. You can also try local or national charities or organisations – for example, a local domestic abuse charity or an anti-bullying organisation.

When choosing external providers, consider:

- Are they adding value to your existing provision?
- What is the background and specialist expertise of the provider?
- Are they skilled and experienced in working with children?
- Do their values align with those of your school?
- Are they promoting a particular viewpoint or political stance?
- Are they recommended by trusted colleagues?
- Have you seen their material? Is it effective RSE? (See Idea 11.)
- Are you able to share their materials with parents?
- How will the input be assessed/evaluated?

Teaching tip

Remember that, while children may enjoy a particular approach or resource, the impact on their learning should be the primary focus. Educational effectiveness should always guide decision-making when bringing in visitors to RSE.

Taking it further

When an external provider is teaching, you should always be in the room with them. Agree beforehand what role you will take in the lesson, and share any key school policies or processes of which they need to be aware. Inform the provider of any additional needs within the group and discuss how these children will be supported.

IDEA 17

Measuring impact

'There's no point in doing RSE if you're not measuring impact.'

Measuring the impact of RSE is essential to ensure that the curriculum is effective in achieving its intended outcomes.

Here are some ways in which to measure the impact of RSE:

- **Parent surveys:** Conduct surveys with parents to gather feedback on your RSE provision.
- **Assessment:** Use assessment to gauge changes in children's knowledge, understanding and skills (see Part 12: Assessment and Evidence).
- **Learning walks:** Observe classroom sessions to assess the quality and effectiveness of RSE (see Idea 18).
- **Feedback from teachers:** Gather feedback from teachers who deliver the RSE curriculum.
- **Behaviour and attitude changes:** Monitor changes in children's behaviour and attitudes. For example, assess whether children demonstrate effective and kind friendship skills.
- **Incidents of bullying and harassment:** Track incidents of bullying, harassment or discriminatory behaviour. A decrease in such incidents can be an indicator of positive change, demonstrating the impact of your RSE programme. A temporary increase could signify that more children are recognising and reporting these behaviours.
- **Case studies and anecdotal evidence:** Collect case studies and anecdotal evidence from children, teachers and parents to highlight specific instances where RSE has made a positive impact on pupils' lives.

Teaching tip

Use a combination of quantitative and qualitative methods to comprehensively assess the impact of your RSE. Put in place processes for ongoing evaluation and monitoring to provide a clear picture of the effectiveness of your RSE and any areas that may need improvement. The impact of your RSE can be shared with staff, parents, governors, inspectors and other interested parties.

Taking it further

Engage RSE consultants, advisory teachers or local authority PSHE leads to conduct independent evaluations of the RSE programme's content, delivery and impact.

IDEA 18

Learning walks

'Learning walks bring RSE to life; they can build confidence by allowing teachers to see others' practice.'

By engaging in learning walks, teachers can observe colleagues' classrooms, gaining insights into different RSE teaching approaches.

Teaching tip

During the learning walk, focus on being an active listener and observer. Make notes to support your reflections..

Taking it further

After the learning walk, analyse the information gathered to support your own or others' development.

Learning walks are mostly carried out by an RSE lead as a means of monitoring RSE delivery across school. However, they can be equally beneficial for teachers looking to develop their own knowledge, skills and confidence.

Choose a focus for your RSE learning walk. Some examples of focus include: content, pedagogy, teaching methods, how a safe learning environment is created, opportunities for children to demonstrate learning, engagement, inclusion, links to British Values, equality and protected characteristics.

Some potential questions to guide the learning walk include:

- How does the teacher create a safe learning environment? Do children feel safe? Why? Why not?
- How does the teaching develop knowledge and skills?
- What activities are used to engage the children? Which work well?
- How do learners with special educational needs and disabilities access the lesson?
- Are there opportunities for children to apply their learning?
- What opportunities are given for children to discuss, reflect and ask questions?
- How well can children articulate what they have learned?
- Are links made to the British Values?
- Are children signposted to support?

Parents

Part 3

IDEA 19

Parent engagement

'There's lots in the media that worries me as a parent, but the staff are always so approachable that it puts my mind at ease.'

Parents are key partners in RSE; learning delivered in school should be followed up and strengthened by parents at home.

In addition to any statutory requirement to consult with parents that may exist in your nation (see Idea 10), look for opportunities to engage with parents on a regular basis to maintain involvement. Below are some ideas to help parents to understand your provision and get involved.

- **Curriculum newsletters and/or knowledge planners:** Inform parents of what is being delivered and when, so that they know what is coming up and can anticipate questions from their child.
- **Newsletters:** Use your newsletter to share updates about RSE – for instance, pictures of learning in RSE, awareness days or links to support for parents.
- **Annual parent survey:** Include a question in your annual parent survey around RSE/PSHE. This will give you valuable data on an ongoing basis to inform your RSE planning.
- **Suggestions box:** Place an RSE suggestions box with slips of paper and a pen in reception and at key events.
- **Dedicated RSE email:** Create a dedicated RSE email address so that parents can email any feedback, suggestions and concerns.
- **Celebration assemblies:** Celebrate children's learning in RSE in an assembly and invite parents along.
- **Stands at parents' evening:** Showcase your RSE provision with a display stand at parents' evening. Share examples of resources and children's work.

> **Teaching tip**
>
> Create a hashtag for your RSE/PSHE content and share pictures of lessons and children's work. Always follow your school's policies and protocols when sharing content and images on social media.

> **Bonus idea** ★
>
> Give parents the chance to view resources at a dedicated meeting or by booking an appointment with a teacher.

IDEA 20

Open-talk café

'As parents, we play a crucial role in shaping our children's understanding of relationships.'

An open-talk café provides a comfortable and supportive environment for parents to explore RSE topics with their children, using storybooks as a focus.

The inspiration for the RSE open-talk café comes from Josie Rayner-Wells, a PSHE consultant based in Norfolk. The aim is to bring children and their parents together to explore RSE topics through stories and related activities.

The first step is to decide on a focus for your open-talk café; examples include puberty, families or friendships. Gather a selection of storybooks on your chosen topic from your school or local library. Choose a date and time for your café and invite parents. (You may want to focus on a particular year group or key stage; younger age groups work particularly well.)

Plan some activities related to your topic. For example, if your books are about families:

- a family tree worksheet
- question cards – 'What is important for our family?', 'What are our values?', 'How do we support each other?'
- a family photo frame template.

On the day, set up an area of school with tables and chairs, refreshments, the books and activities. Invite children to sit with their parents, choose a book to read through and complete the activities.

For a more structured event, choose one book, read it aloud to the parents and children and then invite all participants to complete the same creative activity.

> **Teaching tip**
>
> Use the opportunity of having parents in school to share information about your RSE curriculum and how the books link to what children are learning. Display information about relevant support services for parents and sources of further support on the themes covered.

> **Bonus idea** ★
>
> Involve older children in choosing the theme for the café, planning the event and selecting the books.

IDEA 21

Homework and projects

'We talked about our family and things we do to care for each other. It was a great opportunity to support my daughter's learning.'

You can encourage parents' engagement in RSE by sending learning home. This could be a simple homework task following a lesson or a more in-depth project over a holiday.

Teaching tip

Be mindful of the circumstances of children in your class. If a project could cause stigma or distress, avoid it.

Here are some ideas for home projects:

- **Storybooks:** Send home storybooks linked to the current theme for children to read with their grown-ups.
- **Family discussion:** Ask children to have a discussion with their grown-ups at home and record their answers in their books. For instance, 'Ask your grown-ups at home about their family when they were growing up, what the best thing about being a parent is or who their best friend is.'
- **Family time capsule:** Children create a family time capsule with their family. They plan what to put in it that would represent their family and show what is important to them.
- **Family vision board:** Each member adds images, words or pictures that represent their dreams and aspirations.
- **Family motto:** The family works together to create a motto that represents their family values and beliefs.
- **Puberty items:** Children work with their grown-ups to create a puberty toolkit to support them as they approach the physical and emotional changes of adolescence.
- **Rocks:** The family paints rocks with words or phrases that are important to them.
- **Family surveys:** Children survey their family to find out about behaviours, thoughts and feelings related to the topic. For example, the survey could have questions linked to what they feel is most important in friendships.

Bonus idea ★

Share the results of home projects at an event that parents can attend.

IDEA 22

Parent meetings

'We work closely with our parents to plan and deliver RSE meetings in a way that is accessible to all.'

RSE meetings provide an opportunity for parents to learn more about the RSE policy and curriculum of the school and ask any questions. Parents can be great allies in RSE. However, given the often polarised views around RSE, meetings need to be carefully managed to ensure that everyone has a voice and a safe environment is maintained.

Here are some top tips for parent meetings:

- Be clear on your objectives – are you aiming to inform or consult? The latter suggests views can influence content or processes. If this is not the case, don't bill the meeting as a consultation.
- Ask for questions to be submitted in advance of the meeting – this allows everyone to be heard and gives time to responses.
- Consider the use of an interpreter or translated materials if this is relevant, to ensure access for all parents.
- At the start of the meeting, present some ground rules, including the importance of mutual respect.
- Outline your policy and curriculum in the context of the ethos and values of your school and safeguarding. Explain to parents why RSE is important for pupils.
- Be transparent in sharing your curriculum plan and be open to feedback.
- Share examples of materials to be used for delivery and offer parents the opportunity to view all materials on request.
- Highlight sources of additional support for parents and how they can complement the school's delivery.
- Provide slips of paper and a 'postbox' for parents to share feedback and questions.

Teaching tip

In the event that a parent is disruptive or abusive, refer back to the ground rules. If the behaviour persists, ask the parent to leave or end the meeting.

Taking it further

Offer the opportunity for parents to join a focus or advisory group for RSE. This is particularly useful if there are lots of concerns about the RSE curriculum. The group can provide a bridge between parents and the school. (See Idea 24.)

IDEA 23

Parent workshop

'The workshop gave me ideas of how to start conversations with my child.'

Nurturing relationships with parents is vital to the success of RSE. Many parents lack the knowledge, skills or confidence to talk about relationships and sex with their child. Hosting RSE workshops can help your parents to build on the learning at school within the home setting.

Teaching tip

Ask parents to complete a quick evaluation to measure the impact and identify future support needs.

As a starting point, survey parents to find out the areas with which they would like support. Offer suggestions such as online safety, bullying, puberty or healthy relationships, and leave space for parents to add their own ideas. Ask whether parents prefer face-to-face or virtual sessions (these are useful, as content can be recorded and shared with others) and the time of day that would suit most. These questions could be added to your broader RSE policy and curriculum consultation survey.

Use the survey results to prioritise topics for workshops. Parents may request workshops that you can plan and deliver in-house. Alternatively, contact local organisations who may provide free support. Some ideas are given below:

- local authority PSHE lead or healthy schools team
- local authority public health team
- school nursing service
- police school liaison officers
- charities – domestic abuse, NSPCC, etc.

Here's a suggested outline for a parent workshop on online safety, specifically around grooming and image-sharing:

- Begin with an introduction and aims.
- Cover the benefits and risks of the internet – parents brainstorm ideas and outline any concerns for them.
- What is grooming? (The NSPCC website contains useful information to plan this section.)
- Consider issues that we see in our school – an outline of current trends, apps that children talk about and problems that occur.
- Look at apps that children use and their risks. (The Internet Matters website has guidance on social networking and messaging apps and risks.)
- Cover how to have discussions with your child. (The Barnardo's website has information on how to talk to children about keeping safe online.)
- Provide signposting to support (NSPCC, Internet Matters, Barnardo's, Childnet).
- Allow time for questions.

> **Bonus idea** ★
>
> Survey parents to identify anyone with the expertise to lead a workshop for others. For example, there may be a school nurse or relationship counsellor among the parent body.

IDEA 24

Parent advisory group

'Being part of the group has helped me to understand what RSE is and how it supports my child to be their best self.'

A parent advisory group dedicated to RSE provides a bridge of communication between educators and parents, fosters a partnership approach to RSE, promotes transparency and helps to ensure alignment with the values of the community.

Teaching tip

Be clear on the boundaries in terms of statutory duties and legislation by which schools must abide. While the group may generate lots of ideas, not everything will be able to be implemented, due to adherence to any statutory requirements, time and resources available.

Taking it further

Regularly evaluate the work of the parent advisory group and make adjustments as needed to ensure effectiveness. Keep the broader school community informed of the group's activities and encourage new parents to get involved.

A first step in creating your parent advisory group is to establish need. This may arise from surveys, parental feedback, concerns or a desire to ensure engagement with changes to your RSE provision.

Define the group's objectives and scope, which could involve resource consultation, advocacy, communication, curriculum development or parental support for RSE at home. Develop a set of ground rules to ensure that meetings run smoothly and everyone has the opportunity to share their views.

Recruit a diverse group of parents to be founding members, set clear terms of reference and outline roles within the group. Actively promote the group to encourage broad participation and representation.

Ensure close links and communication with school staff. Include at least one teacher – possibly the PSHE/RSE lead – in the parent advisory group. The PSHE/RSE lead should equip members with ample information, empowering them as advocates for RSE.

Determine initial projects or areas of focus, such as a policy review or gathering parent feedback. Implement clear reporting mechanisms for the group and build in opportunities for them to hear how their views are making a difference within the school.

IDEA 25

Website

'The school website is often the first point of call for existing and prospective parents, community members and school inspectors.'

Your website serves as a vital platform for parents to access information about your RSE policy and curriculum. Transparency and openness are key to building trust and engaging parents in this important area of education.

As a minimum, your website should contain an RSE policy and curriculum section. This may be as part of a broader PSHE area. Clearly outline the topics covered, how you ensure age-appropriateness and the teaching methodologies employed. Explain your school's commitment to providing a safe, inclusive and respectful learning environment for all children. In addition to these, consider including:

- **Links to sources of information:** Include links to support parents to talk to their children about RSE – for example, Parentkind, NSPCC and the NHS.
- **Links to sources of support:** Include links to trusted local and national support agencies – for example, domestic abuse charities.
- **Examples of resources:** Showcase some examples of resources used in different year groups. You could also add a list of suggested books for parents to read with their children to complement the school's provision.
- **Information about awareness days:** Share a calendar of awareness days with a link to relevant websites. Explain the significance and how the school intends to mark them.
- **A bespoke email address for RSE questions and feedback:** This personalised approach demonstrates that the school values parental feedback and actively seeks their engagement. Respond promptly to ensure that parents feel heard.

Teaching tip
Review your website regularly to ensure that it has the most up-to-date information. Amend content based on feedback from stakeholders.

Taking it further
Demonstrate the impact of your RSE by sharing children's work on the website.

Bonus idea ★
Create a hashtag for your RSE or broader PSHE to make it easy for parents to search on social media. Include a social media stream on your website. Encourage parents to use the hashtag when sharing experiences, insights and home learning.

Creating a safe learning environment

Part 4

IDEA 26

Keeping children safe

'If children feel unsafe in RSE, they will not learn effectively.'

Some topics in RSE are sensitive and may provoke a range of thoughts, feelings and reactions for your learners. Creating a supportive learning environment ensures that all children feel safe to participate.

To create a safe space for RSE, consider the following areas:

- **Curriculum:** Deliver a curriculum that is based on the age and stage of learners so that everyone can access the learning. Differentiate appropriately to meet all needs.
- **Group agreement:** Create a group agreement or contract with your class (see Idea 27 for more on creating a group agreement). This provides the rules that children and adults will follow in each RSE lesson.
- **Distancing techniques:** Children may worry that their own feelings or lives will become classroom discussion. By distancing the learning with characters, case studies, scenarios and stories, children can critically analyse, reflect on and empathise with situations, lessening the risk of personal vulnerability and harm.
- **Past experiences or trauma:** Speak with children who may find content challenging – for example, those who have recently experienced a bereavement. Engage with parents to see how best to support the child; this could include going through the lesson individually beforehand, having an opt-out card or doing alternative work outside of the classroom.

> **Teaching tip**
>
> Monitor body language within sessions to ensure that everyone is feeling safe. Use a check-in question with children at different points during the session: 'How are you feeling?'

- **Questions:** Allow opportunities for questions so that children can clarify and extend their learning.
- **Resources:** Choose resources that reflect diversity, are inclusive and do not cause distress. Resources that are hard-hitting and produce a shock reaction in children are not appropriate for learning.
- **Groupings:** Consider how best to group children during RSE. It may be appropriate for some sensitive topics to have children sitting in friendship groups or to give them a choice of seat.
- **Signpost to support:** Discuss in-school and external sources of support in each lesson.
- **Evaluation:** Ask pupils whether they feel safe in lessons and why/why not. Use this to inform planning.

> **Bonus idea** ★
>
> Begin your RSE lessons with icebreakers to help children feel more comfortable and at ease. These encourage openness and foster a sense of security in RSE lessons, making it easier for children to engage in discussions.

IDEA 27

Group agreement

'It was good to make the rules because it meant that everyone will work together well.'

The group agreement is a set of rules developed with children that sets the expectations for behaviour and engagement during RSE lessons.

Teaching tip
Add to or refine the group agreement as lessons progress if needed.

By creating a group agreement with your class, you provide the opportunity for them to explore what keeps them and others safe. It safeguards you as the teacher and cultivates a positive environment where everyone feels safe and included.

A group agreement should be developed in collaboration with your children at the start of the year. Here are some sample approaches:

- In small groups, ask children to brainstorm rules that will help them to learn and keep safe in RSE. Join two groups together to refine their ideas. Continue until you are left with just two sets of rules to amalgamate.
- Give children a set of rules that you have developed (see the examples on the next page). Ask them to think about what each rule means in practice and prioritise which they feel are most important. Take feedback and develop a set that reflects their ideas.

Once developed, the group agreement should be a working document, referenced at the start of and during each lesson. You can encourage children to reflect on their behaviour during the session using questioning, e.g. 'Who is demonstrating our rules well today?' or 'How can we show that we are listening well?'

Here are some sample statements for a group agreement:

- Ask questions, but not personal ones. (This protects you and others from being asked personal questions.)
- Show respect to others.
- Listen well.
- Share your thoughts and views kindly.
- Support everyone to join in.
- Only speak for yourself, using 'I'. (This is to prevent children from speaking about others in the room or outside, e.g. 'My dad says...')
- Keep yourself and others safe. (Talk about confidentiality and how you would need to share if someone is at risk.)
- You can get support from...
- Talk to trusted adults after the session. (You might also choose to include something around children only talking to others in their class or trusted adults about the content, and not younger children.)

Taking it further

Involve children in creating a set of positive affirmations linked to the group agreement. Encourage them to commit to these values both inside and outside of the classroom. This helps them to 'live' the group agreement in their everyday lives.

IDEA 28

Supporting children to access help

'We all need help sometimes.'

The sensitive nature of RSE means that children may need to talk about issues raised with a trusted adult after the session. In RSE lessons, you can give them the knowledge and skills to seek help for themselves and others.

In each lesson, signpost children to sources of support, both inside and outside of school. This could be covered as part of the group agreement, during and/or at the end of each lesson. Periodically, go over who can help in school, outlining those with specific pastoral support roles, while also reinforcing that any staff member in school can help. Encourage children to talk through questions, concerns and worries with grown-ups at home. Also, teach children the Childline number and web address for those who do not feel able to talk with someone in person.

In lessons, explore the reasons why someone might need help from an adult, using discussion, scenarios and stories. Explore the thoughts and feelings of different people who need help. Encourage the children to consider the barriers to seeking help – for instance, embarrassment or fear and how these can be overcome. Reinforce the need to seek help on behalf of a friend if they think that person is at risk of harm.

As well as the knowledge to seek help, children also need the skills. Ensure that there are opportunities for children to develop the skills of assertiveness and articulating their feelings and needs. Practise sentences that children might use to seek help in different situations.

> **Teaching tip**
>
> To support those who feel less comfortable or confident to approach a member of staff in school, implement a system where children can write a note in a book or post a note into a box.

Role-play is a perfect activity for developing these skills.

Teach children regularly about when is the right time for them to contact emergency services and how to do so. This would be when there is not an adult available and they are witnessing or experiencing the following:

- medical emergencies
- fires
- accidents
- crimes
- safety concerns (e.g. they are being followed).

Support children to view seeking help as a strength rather than a weakness, by sharing positive examples of when people have reached out to others.

Taking it further

Invite guest speakers, such as the school nurse or a representative from a local charity, to discuss their roles and how they can help children. This helps to build relationships and break down barriers, helping children become more familiar with sources of support.

IDEA 29

Managing disclosures

'That happened to me.'

The nature of the content and approach to RSE can create an environment where children feel more able to recognise and disclose abuse and other safeguarding concerns. It is important that teachers are prepared to deal with such disclosures in a sensitive way.

Teaching tip

Remind children that they can talk with you in private at any time if they are worried about something.

Taking it further

If a child discloses in front of the whole class, acknowledge them and the importance of what they have said. Explain in a gentle way that you would like to speak with them some more about what they have said, as you recognise that it is important to them.

To prepare yourself for possible disclosures, ensure that you are familiar with your school's safeguarding policy and procedures. All concerns of a safeguarding nature should be referred to your DSL and logged using your school's system.

Clarify boundaries around confidentiality and safety at the start of each session, using your group agreement (see Idea 27). Reinforce that this is a safe space where children are respected. Outline when you would need to speak with a child further and involve others — for example, in the event of a disclosure that a child was at risk of being harmed.

In the event of a disclosure of a safeguarding nature:

- Keep calm and show that you're listening and taking their disclosure seriously.
- Validate the child's feelings.
- Express appreciation for their trust in confiding in you.
- Ask open-ended, non-leading questions to gather essential information.
- Do not make assumptions or judgements.
- Offer support to the child as appropriate within your setting.
- Talk through next steps with the child.
- Document and report the disclosure.
- Practise self-care; seek support from colleagues and debrief if needed.

IDEA 30

SEND

'All children should be able to access RSE appropriate to their needs.'

RSE is a vital subject for all children, but particularly those for whom their additional need or disability makes them more vulnerable to abuse and exploitation. Children with special educational needs and disabilities (SEND) may need a tailored approach to RSE that supports their individual needs and abilities.

An individualised RSE learning plan should be developed for each child with SEND. These plans should outline the needs of the child and how they can be met through, for instance, visual aids, adapted learning materials, repetition, use of signs and symbols, and simplified language. It is useful to involve parents in this process, as they can support in reinforcing learning at home.

The practice of Social Stories™, developed by Carol Gray in 1991 for supporting children with autism, can be particularly useful for exploring key concepts in RSE. There are criteria for creating Social Stories™ on carolgraysocialstories.com (Gray, 2015). Social Stories™ can be utilised to explore concepts such as hygiene, friendships, managing menstruation and public and private behaviour. Each Social Story™ should be tailored for the particular needs of the individual child and answer relevant 'wh' questions.

When delivering RSE, consider the sensory needs of different children. For example, use a range of sensory experiences to deliver information, e.g. tactile materials, visuals and hands-on activities. Be mindful of the noise generated by group discussion and activity-based learning, and how this may be overstimulating for some learners.

Teaching tip

Encourage peer support for children with SEND by using group activities. This develops empathy and understanding and creates an inclusive learning environment that benefits all children.

Taking it further

Continuously review the effectiveness of your provision for pupils with SEND, through pupil voice, parent engagement and feedback from educators.

Bonus idea ★

Consider whether additional sessions with a teaching assistant or SENDCo (SEND coordinator) are needed to enable the child to get the most out of RSE.

IDEA 31

Equality and protected characteristics

'RSE is an excellent vehicle for exploring equality and the protected characteristics.'

Understanding equality and the protected characteristics help to prepare children for life in modern Britain, linking with the British Values. Delivering education around this in RSE allows children the opportunity to explore and develop empathy and to feel valued and safe.

Teaching tip

Being inclusive is as much about how things are delivered as it is about what is taught. Deliver in a balanced and objective way, advocating for the diverse range of people in society.

By ensuring that your provision of RSE is inclusive, you support the creation of a safe learning environment. Every child feels safe because they see themselves and their families represented in the learning.

Before beginning teaching about equality, one of my key recommendations to schools is to examine their provision by looking through the lens of each protected characteristic. For example, if you take the lens of 'age', what do you find out? What messages do your teaching, resources, books and displays give to children about age? Do they perpetuate any stereotypes – for example, older people being wise, frail or grandparents? This will give you areas for development to ensure that your provision is inclusive.

Some schools choose to use imagery to highlight the protected characteristics. While this may support children to recognise and remember them, it's important to ensure that the images used don't unintentionally reinforce stereotypes.

Here are some examples of ways in which you can cover and be inclusive of the protected characteristics through your RSE provision:

- **Age:** Explore stereotypes when discussing different stages of life, e.g. teenager or older person.
- **Disability:** Read books about friendship that feature a child with a disability. Develop empathy through discussion; link this to discussion of being inclusive within friendships.
- **Race:** Include a range of products for different hair types within your puberty box. Focus on racism when exploring bullying.
- **Religion or belief:** Include faith perspectives when exploring sex, marriage and puberty (see Idea 33).
- **Pregnancy and maternity:** Talk about breastfeeding when exploring baby care, and the right to do this in public spaces. Investigate the responsibilities of being a parent.
- **Marriage and civil partnership:** Look at laws around marriage and civil partnership, what marriage and civil partnership are and why people get married or enter a civil partnership. Explore values and commitment.
- **Sex:** Introduce children to names for genitals and how this denotes their sex. Explore stereotypes around sex that can lead to discrimination.
- **Gender reassignment:** Share age-appropriate examples of people who have transitioned, focusing on understanding and compassion.
- **Sexual orientation:** Explore a range of family types, including same-sex parents. Identify the ways in which families are made, including adoption.

Taking it further

Review and allocate RSE fiction books across every year group to ensure each age range has access to materials that appropriately explore protected characteristics. Encourage children to discuss the stories to promote understanding and respect for diversity.

IDEA 32

LGBT

'We want all children and families to feel included in our school.'

RSE should be inclusive of all children and families. Including reference to lesbian, gay, bisexual and transgender (LGBT) people in your RSE content and delivery supports children to become compassionate and accepting members of society who value diversity.

Teaching tip

Use inclusive language that acknowledges a range of family types.

Teaching about LGBT people supports the creation of an equitable, discrimination-free space, in line with the Equality Act 2010.

There are a range of ways in which to include LGBT people in RSE:

- **Families:** When children are learning about families, include a range of family types. Teach children that there are a variety of ways to be a family, but the most important thing is that they love and care for one another.

- **Books:** Use fiction and non-fiction books to explore a range of family types. Children can complete activities based on the books to deepen their understanding (see Idea 46).

- **Awareness days and celebrations:** Use these opportunities as a focus for learning about the experiences of LGBT people – for instance, Anti-Bullying Week, LGBT History Month and World Mental Health Day.

- **Case studies and scenarios:** Include LGBT people in RSE case studies and scenarios. This doesn't have to be the focus of the scenario; for example, in a scenario about a child who is worried about something happening online, the child happens to live with two mums.

- **Gender stereotypes:** If we address gender stereotypes, all children benefit, as we empower them to be themselves and reach their full potential regardless of societal expectations. Ways in which to address stereotypes in RSE include stories that counter traditional stereotypes, encouraging critical thinking about the advertising of products and clothing, and sharing case studies of people who challenge traditional stereotypes.
- **Role models:** Include role models from the LGBT community in your teaching. For instance, when discussing the role of fathers in parenting, use Tom Daley as an example.
- **Sex Education:** Make reference to same sex relationships when exploring sex, contraception and starting a family, e.g. referencing IVF, sperm and egg donation, adoption.
- **Puberty:** Consider your use of language when describing bodies and boy/girl changes, you could use phrases like 'most boys' bodies look like...' or 'for most girls, this is what happens...' so that children who are questioning their gender feel included.

Teaching tip

Ensure LGBT content is woven into the curriculum rather than included as a one-off lesson. This supports children to respect the diversity of society.

IDEA 33

Faith

'We worked with our parent community to explore how to make our RSE more faith-inclusive. Parents are really pleased that our provision now reflects a range of views.'

There are many and varied views around RSE themes, from both a faith and non-faith perspective. It is important for children to have the opportunity to explore these in order for them to appreciate diversity and promote acceptance.

Teaching tip

Reinforce the fact that some values are shared by many faiths, such as respect, kindness and compassion, and could be seen as basic human values.

Taking it further

When exploring diverse perspectives, reinforce your school values and ethos: 'There are lots of different views... not right or wrong, just different' or 'In this school, we believe...'

Work with your parent body to explore what is important for them in terms of faith representation.

Audit your RSE curriculum to identify opportunities to reflect faith practices and perspectives. Due to the differences in interpretation within faiths, you may choose to represent a range of views, rather than linking these to specific faiths. For instance, in some faiths, people believe that sex is part of marriage and should not take place outside of it. Make links between your religious education (RE) curriculum and RSE. Many topics and themes covered in RE will be relevant to RSE.

Other examples of where faith can be reflected as part of RSE include: coming-of-age celebrations in different faiths – for example, confirmation in Christianity, Amrit Sanchar in Sikhism and Bar and Bat Mitzvah in Judaism; talking about pubic hair removal for Muslims in puberty lessons; and arranged marriage.

Where schools share faith perspectives, it is important to also reflect the law as it stands within relationships. For instance, for some people of faith, marriage is celebrated between a man and a woman; the law in this country says that men and women, men and men, and women and women can get married.

Part 5

Preparing to teach

IDEA 34

Assessing training needs

'Completing the needs assessment was a relief, as it allowed me to identify the areas where I was struggling.'

We know that many staff will have received little or no RSE training, which may result in a lack of confidence when delivering. Conducting a needs assessment empowers staff to reflect upon and identify their specific training needs, taking ownership of their professional development in this area.

A needs assessment should be carried out annually to identify training for the coming academic year. Using an electronic survey tool will ease the burden in analysing results.

Here are some sample questions for a training needs assessment:

How knowledgeable are you on...

- statutory requirements for RSE
- resources for teaching RSE
- strategies for answering questions
- what should be taught and when
- the school policy on RSE
- the rationale for RSE
- creating a safe learning environment
- faith perspectives around RSE
- LGBTQ+ inclusion
- The Equality Act?

How skilled are you in...

- teaching sensitive RSE topics
- answering children's questions around RSE
- creating a safe learning environment
- managing discussions
- challenging discriminatory language and behaviour
- choosing and adapting appropriate resources
- differentiating resources for children with SEND
- providing inclusive RSE?

Teaching tip

Reassure staff that the needs assessment is a supportive process, to ensure that they receive the training and development that meets their needs. Share key trends so that staff appreciate that they are not alone.

How confident do you feel to...

- teach about... (include a list of topics)
- answer children's RSE-related questions
- manage discussions
- challenge discriminatory language and behaviour
- choose and adapt resources
- support the needs of children with SEND
- be inclusive of LGBTQ+ people
- have conversations with parents about RSE?

Adding some additional open-ended questions will give staff the opportunity to expand on their answers:

- Do you have any specific questions that you would like answered?
- To enable you to teach RSE confidently, what is your number one request?
- Are there any questions from children that you would find difficult to answer?

> **Taking it further**
>
> As a teacher, you could use the questions on this page to reflect on your own knowledge, skills and confidence to deliver RSE. What are your areas for development?

IDEA 35

Unconscious bias

'Once my awareness was raised, I began to see how my unconscious biases were influencing my practice.'

Being aware of unconscious bias is crucial in order to provide inclusive, balanced RSE to children. Unconscious bias is natural and unintended; however, it means that it is possible for us to treat someone unfairly even when we believe that this is wrong.

Teaching tip

Ask for feedback from colleagues to critique your decisions and practice, to become aware of any biases.

Unconscious bias is when our brains make quick judgements or assumptions about people or situations without us realising it. These can be based on our previous experiences, background, culture and societal stereotypes.

How might unconscious bias impact on RSE?

- **Content and resource selection:** Unconscious biases might influence what a teacher chooses to teach and the resources that they use. For example, some topics might be given less priority, due to the personal biases of the teacher. They may choose resources that do not reflect diversity – for example, only representing one type of family.

- **Tone and language:** Unconscious biases can affect the language used during RSE sessions. Teachers might unintentionally use language or a tone that reinforces stereotypes or discriminates towards certain groups. For example, a teacher might only refer to 'mums' and 'dads' when discussing families.

- **Implicit messaging:** Teachers might unknowingly convey beliefs or attitudes that perpetuate stereotypes related to gender, sexual orientation or relationships. For example, a teacher might focus only on girls when talking about the importance of skincare during puberty, neglecting boys, who may also have skincare needs.

- **Teaching methods:** Teachers might favour certain teaching approaches or examples that align with their biases, potentially excluding or undermining the experiences of some children. For example, a teacher might not give boys the opportunity to handle period products in a lesson because they assume that this will make the girls embarrassed.

- **Interaction with children:** Unconscious biases might affect how a teacher interacts with their class. This could lead to inequality or attention based on stereotypes – for example, assuming that a child follows a particular faith in a set way and therefore asking them to explain more about their perspective every time that faith is mentioned.

How to become aware of unconscious bias:

- Attend a training course to learn more.
- Slow down your decision-making so that you engage your conscious brain.
- Analyse your inner thoughts in certain situations. What are they telling you and why?
- Explore your views about a range of people. What do you believe about them? Is this based on fact or bias?
- Reflect on your decisions and choices. Why did you choose one resource over another?

> **Taking it further**
>
> Unconscious bias is a fascinating area to bring into the RSE curriculum for children.

IDEA 36

Values

'I've realised staff have very different views about relationships, and it's important we all recognise that before teaching.'

Your role in RSE is not to share your values but to provide balanced and non-judgemental teaching that explores a range of views.

Teaching tip

Get into the habit of regularly reflecting on your values so that your teaching remains balanced and inclusive. In order to teach in a non-judgemental and balanced way, you have to be aware of your own values and attitudes.

Values are our beliefs about what is important in life; they are influenced by our upbringing and experiences. Before delivering RSE, consider your own values relating to the topic being explored. For example, what are your views on the following statements – do you agree or disagree?

- Getting married is the biggest commitment that a couple can make.
- Social media is harmful for children.
- Teaching children about RSE helps to empower them.
- Bullies deserve as much sympathy as those who are bullied.
- Sex should take place only within marriage.

Reflect on whether the children in your class may have similar or different values to your own and how your values align – or not – with those of the school.

When teaching RSE, your own values should not guide the content and delivery; what is important is that children are able to appreciate the breadth of values that people might hold, as well as learning facts about such things as the law. Being aware of your own values means that you are more likely to avoid biases when teaching. Once you know what your values are, you can consciously share a range of views and perspectives to increase children's understanding. Through this process, children can safely reflect on their own values and determine whether they serve them well.

IDEA 37

CPD

'Once you stop learning, you start dying.' (Albert Einstein)

Good-quality training and continued professional development (CPD) supports the effective delivery of RSE.

The number of RSE training providers has increased over recent years. This increase makes it more challenging for schools to find an effective provider that meets their needs. Here are some things to consider when choosing a training provider:

- What is their experience and track record?
- Do you have a recommendation from a trusted colleague?
- Can they provide testimonials from other schools/trusts?
- Does their training offer meet your needs? Is there a bespoke option?
- Do they promote a particular value or view? Is this in line with your school ethos and values?
- Do they provide value for money?

Here are some examples of RSE training providers:

- **Local authority (including Public Health England):** Many local authorities have funded training for schools on a range of RSE topics.
- **Teaching school hub:** Your local teaching school hub may provide training and support.
- **PSHE Association:** The professional body for PSHE provides training and networks on a range of topics.
- **Sex Education Forum:** This membership organisation provides networks and training specifically around RSE.
- **Independent consultants:** An independent consultant will offer a range of training solutions based on your needs.

> **Teaching tip**
>
> Link up with another local school to share the cost of some bespoke training.

> **Bonus idea** ★
>
> There are a range of other organisations and charities that offer training around RSE and related themes – for instance, Brook and NSPCC. In addition, many companies who provide teaching schemes will have accompanying training.

IDEA 38

Networking

'It's great to have a community of support, particularly as teaching RSE can have its challenges.'

Engaging with an RSE or PSHE network isn't just about making connections; it's about creating a support system where you can update, share good practice and explore common challenges with like-minded peers.

There are lots of networks that are already established. Good places to look for these include:

- **Local authority:** Many local authorities run PSHE networks for schools and academies in their area. Engaging with a local network has particular benefits, as there may be similar challenges for schools. It also gives you the opportunity to learn more about local support and services.

- **Social media:** There are lots of groups for teachers on Facebook, mainly focused on broader PSHE, with some specific to RSE. Online groups can be really useful for finding out about new resources and how other schools across the country approach RSE. There can be some misinformation on these groups, so keep a critical eye.

- **Other options:**
    - trusts
    - teaching school hubs
    - organisations such as the PSHE Association
    - Larger PSHE resource companies.

If you can't find a network, why not set up your own with some colleagues? I often suggest this to teachers when I've worked with them to develop their practice. It is such a good way to learn from others, as well as to feel good about yourself and your provision!

Teaching tip

Don't be shy to suggest a focus for a network or to volunteer to share your or your school's good practice.

Bonus idea ★

If setting up your own network, having a set agenda/structure for each session can ease the burden of planning. An example structure might be: introductions, updates, sharing of good practice and challenges. Invite visitors to your sessions to share their expertise or RSE offer for schools – for example, the local police school's officers.

IDEA 39

Support

'I sometimes find it quite stressful not knowing what direction a lesson might take based on children's questions and discussions.'

RSE teaching can be daunting and challenging at times, particularly when faced with topics that you find uncomfortable or when managing disclosures from children. Engaging with support can bolster confidence and wellbeing.

Support can take several forms:

- **CPD:** Find and attend specialist RSE training and development opportunities to increase confidence and skills around handling sensitive topics or questions.
- **Keep up to date:** Join mailing lists from key organisations (see Idea 4) to be updated on current research, best practices and age-appropriate resources for teaching RSE.
- **Join a network:** Connect with other teachers, either online or face to face. For instance, this could be via social media, through your trust or local authority, or through a national organisation.
- **Reflect:** Engage in regular reflection to process challenging or sensitive discussions.
- **Establish personal boundaries:** Recognise your own emotional limits. Seek support or ask for assistance from colleagues if a topic or lesson becomes emotionally challenging.
- **Self-care:** Prioritise your own self-care. Engage in activities that promote relaxation, such as exercise, mindfulness and hobbies.
- **Seek support:** Speak to colleagues, your leadership team or school counsellor if you are finding RSE delivery difficult. Explore the option of a debrief session after any difficult topics or lessons.
- **Maintain professional boundaries:** Avoid personal disclosure or biased opinions during sessions.

Teaching tip

Never underestimate the power of positive self-talk. Acknowledge the importance of your role in facilitating RSE and celebrate successes and positive outcomes.

Taking it further

If there is a topic that you know you will find challenging due to personal circumstances, speak with a trusted colleague.

IDEA 40

Improving knowledge

'It's hard to keep up to date with the knowledge required to deliver effective RSE.'

Teaching RSE requires a balance of knowledge, empathy and communication skills. While you don't have to be an expert in all areas to deliver RSE, feeling knowledgeable increases confidence and allows you to deepen the children's learning.

Teaching tip

Sign up to relevant mailing lists to receive regular updates.

There are lots of sources of information; an important aspect of developing knowledge is the ability to critically appraise these.

Firstly, check the credibility and credentials of the organisation and author supplying the information; are they reputable and recognised in the field of RSE? Do they base their practice on research and evidence? Do they cite reliable sources of evidence?

Cross-reference any information with other reputable sources to check for consistency. If multiple sources use the same statistics or give similar advice, this adds to the credibility of the information.

Evaluate whether the information is presented objectively or whether it appears to have an agenda or bias, to ensure objectivity. Sources that are over-promotional or one-sided might have a financial or ideological bias.

Here are some sources of factual information for you to appraise:

- **www.nhs.uk:** The NHS website gives factual information about a range of health areas, including puberty, periods, acne, pregnancy and vaginal discharge.

- **www.ceopeducation.co.uk:** This provides a wealth of information for professionals around online safety and sexual exploitation from the Police Child Exploitation and Online Protection Command.

- **www.anti-bullyingalliance.org.uk:** This site has resources and information about bullying, plus it's the home of Anti-Bullying Week.
- **www.nspcc.org.uk:** This provides information for professionals on healthy sexual development, abuse and safeguarding.
- **www.mentallyhealthyschools.org.uk:** From the Anna Freud mental health charity, this includes research and resources around mental health.
- **www.forwarduk.org.uk:** This site provides guidance and knowledge about female genital mutilation.
- **www.womensaid.org.uk:** This organisation provides information and support about domestic abuse.
- **www.citizensadvice.org.uk:** This site contains a detailed section on marriage and civil partnerships.
- **www.equalityhumanrights.com:** This provides an overview of equality laws and protected characteristics.

Taking it further

Use a virtual pinboard, such as Padlet, to organise links to organisations and important sources of RSE-related information. Share with colleagues and ask them to add to it.

IDEA 41

Key messages

'Our key messages help to ensure consistency across our RSE provision.'

Developing a set of key messages for RSE helps you to reinforce learning and answer questions.

Key messages are a way of sharing the ethos and values your school wants to promote in relation to relationships and sex. People hold diverse values and attitudes; having key messages ensures that everyone in school is on the same page.

Ideally, key messages will be developed in consultation with all staff and parents, in line with the RSE policy. Select key RSE topics and brainstorm the messages that you would like all children to have about these. Narrow down the choices to three or four key messages that you will promote through the delivery of RSE. Here are some example key messages:

Families
- There is no 'right' way to be a family; they come in all shapes and sizes.
- Families are built on love and care.

Consent
- Your body belongs to you; no one should touch you in a way that makes you feel uncomfortable.
- It's OK to change your mind.

Friendship
- Friends respect your space.
- Friends are kind to one another.

Inclusion
- Our school welcomes everyone.
- In our school, everyone has equal value.

Teaching tip

Display key messages in your classroom.

Taking it further

You might decide to have different key messages per year group or key stage. Reinforce your key messages during lessons and use them to guide your answers to children's questions.

Part 6

Being creative with RSE delivery

IDEA 42

Participatory RSE

'When you start to develop your powers of empathy and imagination, the whole world opens up to you.' (Susan Sarandon)

A key part of RSE pedagogy is using participatory techniques. This not only makes RSE more fun and engaging for children, but it also contributes to the development of skills and increases opportunities to hear others' views.

Teaching tip

Be clear from the beginning and throughout what the learning points are for the activity, so that children don't get too carried away with the fun. Encourage reflection afterwards to reinforce the learning.

There are many benefits to using participatory activities such as art and drama to deliver your RSE.

- **Teacher as observer:** When children are engaged in group activities, it allows you to observe and listen to their discussions. This is a great way in which to assess where the children are at.

- **Engagement:** Something slightly different to the 'normal' way of working has the potential to keep children engaged and focused.

- **Skills development:** Children practise skills as they engage in the activity – for example, team-working skills, listening, negotiating or decision-making.

- **Accessible:** There are fewer barriers to participation for those who struggle with reading and writing.

- **Empathy:** Participatory activities, particularly those involving drama or scenarios, allow opportunities for children to practise their empathy and to consider the views and experiences of others.

- **Exploration:** There are fewer opportunities for failure in creative activities, and this may increase children's desire to explore and be curious.

IDEA 43

Drama techniques

'Drama offers a safe way to try ideas as a practice for real life.'

Using drama techniques provides a great opportunity to explore feelings, motivations and the consequences of actions. Children develop empathy by seeing things from someone else's perspective.

In **hot-seating**, one person becomes a character and takes questions from the rest of the group. This could be a character from a book, film or a scenario that you have created. For example, you are doing some work around change and transition, so you ask a confident child to play Kavita, who is moving to a new school and wants advice. The children share ideas with Kavita about what she could do to make friends.

In **still image**, ask children to create a 'freeze-frame' picture to demonstrate a word or phrase – for instance, 'family', 'kindness', 'sharing' or 'conflict'. Share the still images with the rest of the class and ask them to discuss what they see. Ask them to guess what each character is thinking or feeling. Still images can also be developed into small dramas.

Forum theatre is a technique developed by Augusto Boal, where the audience takes an active role in the drama and can influence the ending. To set up forum theatre, firstly task children with creating role-plays or small dramas (see Idea 96). For example, one person is pressurising their friend to break the rules. Once the role-plays/dramas are created, one group presents to the class. The audience is told that at any point they can stop the action and give advice to the characters on what they could do next. Children explore how a character's actions and behaviours can change the outcome of situations.

Teaching tip

Encourage children to make their drama as true to life as possible, but not so real that they are using actual events or people. Be clear on the boundaries when using drama; give a start and end signal for children to go into and come out of role.

Taking it further

Develop scenarios to show in assembly, to teach other children in school.

Bonus idea ★

Get into the hot seat as an 'expert', a person wanting information or someone with a dilemma. For example, play an alien from outer space who is visiting earth to find out about families – what can the children tell you?

IDEA 44

Continuum

'I listened to what Jordan said and changed my mind.'

A key part of RSE is exploring children's attitudes and values. Using a continuum is a great way in which to do this. It allows children to express their own views while hearing and potentially learning from the views of others.

Here are some activities that I like to use to explore attitudes and values in RSE.

Statements continuum

Children decide whether they agree or disagree with certain statements. Firstly, create a set of statements based on the RSE topic that you are exploring. For example:

- 'Trust is the most important quality in a friendship.'
- 'It is easy to talk about puberty.'

There are a range of ways in which this activity can be delivered:

- Children work individually or in groups to decide whether they strongly disagree, disagree, agree or strongly agree with a number of statements on a worksheet.
- The statements are pinned around the room; children work their way around them, putting a mark with a pen where they sit on the continuum.
- You read out the statements and children make a sign (e.g. hands up or down) or move to a certain area in the room to show their answer.

Once children have made their choices, discuss them as a class. Feed in diverse views and play 'devil's advocate' as appropriate, to encourage deep thinking. Let children know that they can change their mind if they hear something with

> **Teaching tip**
>
> When exploring attitudes, there is no right or wrong answer. Be careful to ensure that no child feels shame for what they believe.

which they agree. Explore why there are so many different views and values.

Sorting

Sorting items is another great way in which to explore children's views, attitudes and values. There are a range of ways to do this:

- Create a 'washing line' from one side of the classroom to the other. Ask children to suggest friendship qualities and write these on sheets of paper. Designate one end of the line to be least important and one end to be most important. Walk along the line with each quality, one at a time, asking children to shout 'stop' when they think that it is in the right place. Once all are positioned on the line, ask whether anyone would like to move the position of a quality. Explore why children might have different views about friendships, stressing that we are all unique and have our own needs.
- Carry out the washing line activity with cards in table groups. There are lots of opportunities for sorting – for instance, best to worst or least to most. An example could be sorting baby items from least to most useful.

The most important part of this activity is the discussion that children have in groups or as a class to highlight the reasons behind people's choices.

Taking it further

Encourage children to identify the attitudes and values of fictional characters through stories and discussion. This can generate discussion about empathy, diversity, and the impact of values on behaviours and actions. It also helps children to reflect on their own beliefs.

IDEA 45

Scenarios

'Scenarios are so versatile and really get children engaged, thinking and discussing.'

I love using scenarios in RSE. They are perfect for exploring emotions, relationships, personal boundaries and decision-making. Scenarios allow children to develop empathy as they consider the feelings of those involved.

Write simple scenarios that are appropriate for the age and maturity of your class. You could use scenarios based on stories or things in the news, but avoid using scenarios that are too similar to real-life events in school, as this may be counterproductive.

Here are some example scenarios:

1. Friendship scenarios

- Ellie's friend wants to play with a different group of people at break. How does Ellie feel? What should Ellie do?
- Jayden and Malik are best friends, but they have had an argument. What can they do to make up and be friends again?

2. Feelings scenarios

- Maryam feels sad because her dog, Rosa, is unwell. What can she do to feel better, and who can she talk to?
- Archie is worried about making friends at his new school. What could he do?

3. Personal boundaries scenarios

- Jakub is uncomfortable when someone invades his personal space. What should he say or do to protect his boundaries?
- Florence doesn't want to share her toys. How can she explain her feelings to her friend?

> **Teaching tip**
>
> Highlight the fact that there is not just one answer to these scenarios; people will have different ideas and that is OK.

4. Family scenarios

- Mia's parents are splitting up. How can she explain this to her friend?
- Max is adopted and wonders about his birth parents. How can he ask his parents about his adoption?

5. Consent scenarios

- Zofia wants to borrow her friend's pen. What should she do to ask for permission?
- Sam wants to join a game that his friends are playing. How can he make sure that he has their consent to join?

6. Body awareness scenarios

- Grace notices that her body is changing as she gets older. Who can she talk to about these changes?
- Mohammad has questions about the differences between boys and girls. Where can he find accurate information?

7. Online safety scenarios

- Nia received a message from someone that she knows online asking her to meet up with him. What should she do to stay safe?
- Caleb wants to share a picture with his friends. How can he ensure that it's appropriate to share online?

Ask children to discuss scenarios in small groups and then take feedback. Encourage children to think about the feelings of the characters involved.

> **Taking it further**
>
> Children could write a follow-up to the scenario to show what happened next.

IDEA 46

Stories

'Through the characters, children were able to empathise with people in very different situations to their own.'

Stories are an accessible way in which to explore RSE topics for a range of age groups in primary.

Teaching tip

Utilise your local library to access a range of books. You can search for themed books on the Book Trust website. Social media platforms can also provide useful information about relevant books for RSE.

Taking it further

To explore a story, you can use questions, such as: What else could they do? What would you advise? How do they/others feel? What will happen next?

Most stories are based around some kind of relationship, whether with self or others. This makes them particularly useful for exploring key themes in RSE. For instance:

- breaking down gender stereotypes
- recognising that families come in all shapes and sizes
- friendship problems
- loss and bereavement
- bullying.

Stories can be used in circle time as a stimulus for discussion around a certain topic. Stories can also be utilised in a more structured way, with activities to meet the outcomes within a lesson:

- Explore the character's feelings at different points.
- Write to one of the characters.
- Give advice to a character at a particular point in the story.
- Act out parts of the story with role-play or puppets.
- Create a new ending.
- Write a diary for the character(s).
- Create still images of key parts of the story – analyse the character's feelings and motivations.

One of the key benefits of using stories is the opportunity for children to develop their skills of empathy, by exploring the experiences of the characters and putting themselves in others' shoes.

Bonus idea ★

Children could try creating a sequel to the story.

IDEA 47

Conscience Alley

'A great way to enable students to practise decision-making and consider influences.'

Conscience Alley is an activity that engages children in thoughtful decision-making and moral dilemmas.

Choose a scenario or decision relevant to your topic and the age of children in your class. Here are some examples:

- Cayla's friend shares a secret with her and tells her not to tell anyone.
- Yihan has a friend online who wants to meet in person.
- Amira's friend wants her to have a sleepover, but Amira doesn't want to.

Divide the class into two groups and explain that they are going to create a pathway. One group will be giving helpful thoughts and influences, and the other unhelpful ones. Allow children time to brainstorm sentences or phrases they might say to the character in the scenario.

Create a physical 'alley' in your classroom, with pupils from each group facing each other and a pathway in between. Identify one pupil to be the character featured in the scenario, who will walk along the 'alley' and hear all the different ideas. If there is time, repeat the activity, with other children taking the part of the character.

Conclude the activity with a debriefing session. Include some of the questions below:

- Did you discover any new ideas that you hadn't thought of before?
- Were there any times when you were unsure about what the right decision might be?
- What did you learn about decision-making?
- What is important when making decisions?
- How did it feel to be in the Conscience Alley?

Teaching tip

Encourage children to consider a range of different perspectives, feelings and consequences of different decisions.

Taking it further

Ask children to imagine how the scenario would play out depending on the decision made. They could do this as a story or a piece of drama, individually or in groups.

IDEA 48

Mood boards

'It was really interesting listening to the children discuss their ideas and observing how they chose images and words to represent these.'

A mood board is a visual presentation featuring images and words. In RSE, mood boards offer a creative way in which to explore topics.

Teaching tip

Remind children to include everyone's ideas on their mood board.

Taking it further

This activity would be most effective once children have done some work around a topic. It could be used as a formative or summative assessment.

Bonus idea ★

Display the mood boards in the classroom or another space in the school.

Collect together large sheets of paper, age-appropriate magazines, printed words, fabrics, stickers, image print-outs, coloured pens and glue.

Decide on a theme for the mood boards related to your current RSE topic – for instance, healthy relationships, stereotypes, online safety, consent or parenting.

Explain to the class what a mood board is and explore the theme. Tell children that the purpose of the activity is to communicate their ideas about the theme to the rest of the class. Ask them what sorts of images and words might represent the theme well.

In small groups, task children with planning and creating their mood board using the materials available to them. With older learners, encourage them to research using books or the internet.

Once all mood boards are complete, ask children to present their mood board to the rest of the class and talk through their ideas. Use questioning to deepen learning:

- What has this activity told us about...?
- Why is it important that children learn about...?
- What are the similarities and differences in the mood boards?
- What are the key messages?
- What skills did you use in this activity?

IDEA 49

Props

'Oooh, I love those. Where did you get them from?'

Props provide a great hook to draw children into discussion or activities in RSE.

Teachers can be so creative, and schemes used to deliver RSE often underuse this key skill. Here are a few of my favourite props and how I use them:

- **Small plastic trash cans:** These can be used for children to sort through relationship behaviours and 'throw away' any unhelpful ones.

- **Cardboard people cut-outs:** These have a multitude of uses, including brainstorming the changes of puberty, exploring feelings or creating characters for a scenario.

- **Painted stones:** I have some with relationship qualities written on them. In groups, children choose a stone and create a still image of the relationship quality shown.

- **Beach balls:** Write on quiz questions and throw them to different children in the class to answer.

- **Playing cards:** I use these to explore status and power in relationships. Each child is given a card and told that the Ace has the lowest status and the King the highest. I present them with a scenario and ask them to interact with one another according to their status.

- **Play money:** This is useful for exploring simple budgeting, e.g. for a baby or for puberty items.

- **Family maths counters:** Ask children to create the ideal family using the counters; explore their choices. Lead into questions around the diversity of families.

Teaching tip

Be creative! Look around your classroom and get inspired.

Bonus idea ★

Look around your classroom. Is there an existing resource used in another subject that you can reuse in RSE? Poundland, Home Bargains and Flying Tiger often have a range of toys and stationery items that can be used as props. Stones from your garden or purchased from a garden centre can be painted and drawn or written on.

IDEA 50

Sculpture

'I'm amazed at the sculptures they created. I was concerned that they wouldn't know what to create, but the results are impressive.'

Creating sculptures in RSE gives children the opportunity to discuss and explore their ideas about different themes in a creative way, while the teacher observes.

Teaching tip

Resist the temptation to give ideas to the children; allow each group to come up with ideas themselves.

Taking it further

During the activity, circulate the groups and listen to their discussions, picking up on thoughts and feelings. This is a great opportunity for you to assess children's views, attitudes and knowledge.

Using sculpture allows children to explore a particular topic without constraints. This activity is as much about the process as it is about the finished result.

Choose a medium for the children to sculpt with – for example, play dough, pipe-cleaners, foil, salt-dough, LEGO® or paper and tape.

Divide the class into groups and give them a phrase or theme to sculpt. For example:

- a happy family
- a healthy friendship
- love
- bullying.

Ask the children to create a sculpture to represent the word or phrase. They should work as a group, making sure that everyone's ideas are considered. They can make a sculpture that is abstract or more realistic. Allow enough time for each group to create their sculpture.

Once all sculptures are complete, ask each group to share and discuss their sculpture. Ask children to highlight similarities and differences between the sculptures. Use questioning to promote deep thinking:

Bonus idea ★

Photograph sculptures and ask each group to write their thoughts around the sculpture as a form of assessment.

- How did you decide on your sculpture?
- What skills did you use in your group?
- What does this tell us about...?
- Why are the sculptures different?
- Why are the sculptures similar?
- How would the sculpture be different if...?

IDEA 51

Puppets

'The children were really invested in the puppet and wanted to help.'

Puppets can be used to support skills development in RSE, as well as to explore more sensitive aspects of the curriculum.

Puppets are a useful tool in RSE, particularly with younger children. They provide a more accessible way to role-play for children with less confidence. They distance the learning so that children can safely explore ideas and themes without using their own experiences.

Here are some ways in which puppets can be used in RSE:

- As teacher, use the puppet to share a problem or dilemma for the children to help with. For example, the puppet is being left out of a friendship group and is feeling sad. They seek advice from the children, through whispering in your ear and you relaying their words.
- Children could use puppets to represent the characters from a story related to an RSE theme – for example, friendship or family issues, loss or bereavement, or being new to a school. They can replay the story with the puppets, make up a new ending or tell one of their own.
- To develop a particular skill, give children a scenario to act out with their puppets – for example, making a new friend, saying no to someone, asking for help or solving a disagreement. Give time for the children to role-play with their puppets. Discuss what techniques they used and how well they worked.

Teaching tip

As with any role-play, be clear on the start and finish of the puppet role-plays and encourage children to think about what might happen in real life.

Taking it further

Children create their own puppets using lolly sticks and masking tape or wooden spoons. This gives them ownership of the characters and allows them to consider what the person looks like and how they present themselves.

IDEA 52

Crafts

'We decorated mirrors with positive friendship messages and hung them in the trees for parents to see as they picked up their children.'

Craft activities offer an opportunity for children to reflect on their learning, while engaged in a creative task.

Teaching tip

Take inspiration from junk – reuse and recycle items for your craft activities if possible.

Taking it further

Display the crafts for members of the school community to see.

What I love most about using craft activities is that it gives you the chance to observe and listen to children's discussions as they are involved in the task. It's a great way to encourage reflection, and supports children to learn from others in the class. Here are some RSE craft ideas:

- **Friendship bracelets:** Following on from learning about friendships, children create friendship bracelets for an allocated person in the class. As they are creating, ask children to talk about the qualities of a good friend.
- **Journals:** Each child decorates a journal (exercise book or handmade book) in which to record their feelings.
- **'I am special' mirror:** Purchase child-friendly mirrors. Children decorate them and include positive affirmations to support their self-esteem.
- **Decorate question boxes for each table:** Talk about why questions are important and highlight the need for privacy.
- **Friendship banner:** Produce a whole-class friendship banner featuring words and pictures linked to friendship.
- **Compliment chain:** Each child decorates a slip of paper with a compliment. These are fastened together to produce a paper chain.
- **Masks showing different emotions:** Individuals decorate masks with different emotions. They use these to discuss the feelings that people might have in relationships.

IDEA 53

Pupil action

'Children loved hearing about the residents lives'.

Including 'pupil action' activities supports skills development and allows children to apply their learning in a real-life context.

These activities allow children to actively increase and consolidate their learning.

Planning an event

Children work together to plan an event linked to RSE – for instance, a parent event linked to an annual awareness day/week, such as Anti-Bullying Week. In groups, children research the subject and plan the event, including publicity materials, an agenda and activities. In doing so, they develop relationship skills of teamwork and communication, while also gaining more knowledge about the topic.

Going to a care home

Children visit a local care home to share care packages and talk to residents. In advance of the visit, children research what would be suitable to include in a care package to meet the needs of an older person. They also think of questions that they might like to ask the residents about their lives. This activity supports children's understanding of life stages, develops their compassion and highlights the importance of maintaining relationships through life.

Caring for a 'baby'

Children are given the opportunity to care for a 'baby' doll for a day or longer. In pairs or groups, children assume the role of parents and become responsible for meeting the needs of the 'baby'. This activity supports children to understand the responsibilities of parenthood, as well as developing skills of caring, effective communication and decision-making.

Teaching tip

Highlight to children the skills that they are using when carrying out these activities.

Taking it further

All these activities should be followed by a debrief to explore the knowledge and skills used and/or gained.

Part 7

Gender, bodies and safety

IDEA 54

Language and terminology

'Oh, there's that one like a place in America... Virginia!'

Using medical or scientific words for genitals helps to develop a common language and understanding in the classroom.

I find that one of the areas of RSE that causes most concern is terminology to describe genitals. Over time, children become more comfortable and confident using scientific language, which will support discussions in later life with medical practitioners and potential intimate partners.

Here are some tips on using scientific language:

- As a staff group, decide on what terms will be used when. Ideally, children will be introduced to some scientific words early in Key Stage 1. Make decisions on which terms will be used in each year group. For example, you may decide only to describe the external genitals (vulva, penis and testicles) in Reception and Year 1.
- When introducing the language to children, explain that some people may feel uncomfortable with these words. Explore scenarios when it would and wouldn't be appropriate to use them.
- Be consistent with all staff modelling the language, including lunchtime supervisors. For instance, if a child hurts their genitals in a game at lunchtime and approaches a lunchtime supervisor, they will use the scientific language as appropriate for the age of the child.
- Reassure parents and children that it is OK for them to continue to use their own words at home, but in school the scientific words will be used. Avoid the term 'correct terminology', as this suggests a value judgement.

Teaching tip

In terms of safeguarding, it is important that children learn the scientific terminology so that they can make trusted adults aware if anyone is touching them inappropriately. Where euphemisms are used, this can mean that opportunities to safeguard are missed.

Taking it further

Many families use euphemisms to describe genitals and may feel uncomfortable with schools introducing the scientific words. Include this in your consultation with parents.

Bonus idea ★

List terminology in your knowledge planners or individual lesson plans.

IDEA 55

Naming genitals

'We call it "bits".'

In this activity, anatomically correct dolls are used to introduce the names for genitals and to explore gender and stereotypes.

Share two anatomically correct clothed dolls with the children, presenting them as two babies that you are looking after. Explain that you are unsure whether the babies are boys or girls. In my experience, children will focus on what they can see on the outside – for instance, 'It's a girl because it's wearing a pink dress' or 'It's a boy because it doesn't have a headband.'

Ask the children: 'When a baby is born, how does the doctor or nurse know whether the baby is a boy or a girl?' Explain that the way the doctor knows is to look between the legs at the 'private' parts. Boys have a penis and testicles and girls have a vulva. Boys wee through a tube that runs through the centre of their penis and girls wee through a small opening in their vulva.

Questions to ask in the discussion:

- Why do people call these 'private parts'? Explore rules around privacy and safe and unsafe touch.
- What other names do you know for these parts of the body? Explore words that children use at home or have heard.

Other ways to introduce vocabulary for genitals:

- Use the NSPCC Talk Pants campaign materials.
- Draw several large body outlines and designate 'boy' and 'girl'. Ask children to label different parts of the body. Use as an opportunity to introduce scientific names for genitals.

Teaching tip

Discuss when children might use the words 'penis', 'testicles' and 'vulva'. For example, they might use those terms in a discussion at school or when asking for help if they have hurt that part of their body.

Taking it further

Read age-appropriate picture books about body parts and privacy.

IDEA 56

Body safety and consent

'I always ask before I hold Cohen's hand and wait for him to say yes or no, because that's consent.'

Teaching about consent and body safety should be a core part of RSE in all year groups.

Teaching tip

Ensure that a safe environment is created before discussing non-consensual touch, and remind children of whom they can talk with if they need help.

Taking it further

Create posters sharing key messages around consent.

Introduce children to the concept of consent when they start school, through teaching the importance of asking for permission before engaging in physical contact, sharing toys, hugging or joining in games.

Build on this in later years when exploring safe and unsafe touch, consent and body autonomy. To illustrate these key concepts, use a puppet (or multiple puppets) as a prop to explore scenarios involving non-consensual touch. Introduce the puppet to the class: 'This is Sam. Sam has a problem that they need your help with.' Explain that Sam is shy and will use you to talk to the class. Sam whispers their problem to you. Relay Sam's problem to the children and ask them to offer advice.

Problems around non-consensual touch might include: a child holding Sam's hand when Sam doesn't want them to, a babysitter who sits too close and touches their hair, a family friend who always hugs them when they don't want to hug or a relative who always gives them a kiss on the cheek when they don't like it.

Focus the children on the characters' feelings in the situation to practise empathy. Address potential obstacles, like the fear of upsetting someone, while emphasising the most appropriate actions to take in each situation.

As children progress and reach the top year groups, they can explore relevant scenarios in small groups. Share their responses as a whole class and draw out key messages.

IDEA 57

Breaking stereotype boxes

'There's no such thing as boys' stuff and girls' stuff; we can do anything.'

In this activity, children learn about gender stereotypes and how they can prevent people from living their best lives and reaching their full potential.

Prepare two large boxes, one labelled 'girls' and one 'boys'.

Begin with a discussion with the class about what they think boys and girls are supposed to do or be like. Encourage them to share their thoughts about toys, colours, clothing, jobs and activities associated with boys and girls.

In small groups, ask children to list the activities, traits or interests that they think are most associated with boys and girls on separate slips of paper. One group at a time, ask the children to drop their slips into either the 'boys' box or the 'girls' box and to describe them as they do so. With younger children, have items and images ready-prepared for them to decide which box they feel that they belong in.

Once all groups have finished, discuss the contents of each box. Take out some slips and ask questions based on what is written, such as 'Can boys also like playing with Barbies?' or 'Can girls enjoy playing Fortnite?' Encourage discussion about how everyone is different and interests are not limited by gender.

Ask children why you have asked them to put the slips into the boxes labelled 'boys' and 'girls' – what do the boxes symbolise? Explain that they symbolise gender stereotypes. Talk through how these stereotypes are damaging, as they can prevent people from doing what really makes them happy and what they enjoy – it keeps them in a 'box'.

Teaching tip

As an added visual representation, you could end the session by breaking the boxes!

Taking it further

Introduce the concept that there are no rules for what boys and girls should like or do. Invite the children to think of activities, hobbies or traits that they enjoy and which might not align with the stereotypes.

Bonus idea ★

Explore how we can break down these stereotypes; talk about the importance of challenging them and not feeling limited by them.

IDEA 58

Personal space

'This is such an important area of learning for our children; the activity really helped them to understand the concept.'

Learning about personal space is a key relationship skill. Demonstrate personal space using a variety of different-sized circles.

Teaching tip

Reinforce the group agreement and allow children to opt out if they feel uncomfortable at any point.

Create three circles of different sizes on the floor; you could use chalk, rope or hoops.

Give children a simple explanation of personal space. For example, personal space is like an invisible bubble around you. It's the area around your body where you feel comfortable and safe. When someone comes too close to you and gets inside your bubble without permission, it can make you feel uncomfortable. We might feel comfortable having some people closer than others. We all have different-sized bubbles around us.

Explain that the circles on the floor represent personal space bubbles. Choose a character from a book or film with which children are familiar. Use a doll or model to represent that character. Read out the scenarios below and ask children to decide which personal space bubble the character might be in when faced with each scenario. Explore any differences of opinion.

- talking with their friend
- playing with their brother or sister (or another close relative)
- a child they don't know asks whether they can play with them at the park
- waiting in a queue at a shop.

Use questions to increase children's understanding of personal space:

- How do we respect other people's personal space? Ask whether they feel OK, not get too close, ask permission.
- What signs might we get if we invade someone's personal space? Explore verbal and body language.
- How does it feel if someone has invaded our personal space? Uncomfortable, scary, weird.
- How can we ask someone to give us more space? Say how you feel, use assertive language.
- Why might we feel OK with some people being closer than others? Trust, the relationship we have with them, family.

Taking it further

Ask children to develop short scenarios demonstrating children respecting one another's personal space.

IDEA 59

Female genital mutilation (FGM)

'It feels a bit of a scary subject for primary age; we don't want to upset them.'

Female genital mutilation is a topic that requires a considered and sensitive approach. Some schools may choose to deliver a specific lesson on FGM if they have children who may be at risk from this practice (see the UK government website for more information on FGM). Others may feel that their existing education around body safety and consent meets the needs of their pupils.

Teaching tip

Reassure children that harmful practices such as FGM are not common, and laws are there to protect everyone.

Before beginning teaching about FGM, ensure that you have undertaken specific training, particularly around how to manage disclosures.

Here are some ideas for educating children about body safety and FGM:

- Choose age-appropriate books that touch on themes of body safety, consent and respecting others. Read the story together and facilitate a discussion on the topic, allowing children to share their thoughts and feelings.
- Teach children about their bodies' autonomy and boundaries. Use simple diagrams or dolls to explain private body parts and discuss the importance of respecting these areas.
- Create posters promoting body safety and respect for others. Display these posters around the school or community to spread awareness.
- Use specific lessons designed to explore FGM. These are available from the National FGM Centre and the PSHE Association.

- Set up scenarios where children act out being supportive friends to someone feeling worried or uncomfortable about a situation. Encourage them to find ways in which to help, and identify when it is necessary to seek adult support.
- Explore the concept of human rights and how everyone deserves to be safe and healthy. Use simple language to illustrate how some practices might violate these rights. For example: In some places, including the UK, some girls might face a harmful practice called female genital mutilation (FGM). This is when a part of a girl's vulva is hurt in a way that causes a lot of pain and affects their health. Even though it's not allowed and it's against the law in the UK, some people still do it because of a tradition. But it's important to know that it's not safe or healthy for anyone. Everyone has the right to be safe and healthy, and hurting someone's body is not OK. People in the UK are working together to stop this and make sure that every girl grows up feeling safe and healthy. If you have more questions, you can always ask a grown-up you trust, like a teacher or a parent.
- Explore support networks and trusted adults. Encourage children to identify whom they can talk to and when it might be appropriate to do so.
- Teach children simple phrases or actions that they can use to express discomfort or to seek help in challenging situations.

Taking it further

Involve parents in conversations about FGM by sharing your approach to teaching body safety and consent. Hold a workshop session to explain how you address sensitive topics, reinforcing the importance of creating a supportive environment for children to ask questions and express their feelings.

IDEA 60

Transgender

'We explore transgender identities in a sensitive way as part of our learning around diversity and inclusion.'

Use a celebrity example to explore transgender identities with primary-age children, encouraging understanding and respect.

Teaching tip

Establish a common definition for the term 'transgender' with colleagues across the school, so that children are getting the same information.

Introduce the concept of celebrities and how they impact on their fans and wider society. Tell the children that sometimes celebrities share personal stories that can help people to understand different experiences. Share some recent examples.

Select a suitable celebrity that the children may know who has openly shared that they are transgender. Ensure that their story is age-appropriate and positive. Share relevant information about the celebrity's journey.

Ask questions to stimulate thinking and discussion:

- Have you heard of this celebrity before?
- How do you think that they felt at different parts of their story?
- How can we show kindness and respect to people who may be different from us?
- How could you support someone going through a similar journey?

Give a definition of transgender and explore how laws protect people from discrimination and abuse.

Finish by reinforcing the importance of respect, kindness and acceptance towards others, including those with different experiences or identities to ourselves.

Part 8

Healthy relationships

IDEA 61

Friendship gardens

'A simple analogy but it really helped my class to explore friendships.'

In this activity, the analogy of a growing garden is used to explain how to nurture and maintain friendships.

Teaching tip

The practical activity of planting the seeds adds a lot to this activity; however, the analogy could be used without this element if needed.

Taking it further

Children can keep journals tracking the progress of their seeds and making comparisons to the growth of a friendship.

Tell children that they are going to create a friendship garden. Give each child or group of children pots, soil and fast-growing seeds, such as sunflowers or poppies. If this activity is done at the start of the school year, it gives more time for the children to see their plants grow. Support children to plant their seeds in the pots. Discuss how to look after their seeds to encourage growth.

Ask the children how the process of growing a seed is similar to the start of a friendship. Explore the children's ideas and use the analogies below to explore the similarities:

- Seeds represent the beginning of a friendship. Like seeds, a friendship starts small, with two people not really knowing one another. Seeds need to be planted and tended to grow; this is the same as two people forming a connection and starting to build their friendship.
- Seeds need water and sunlight to grow. A friendship needs care and attention in order to develop. Spending time together, being kind and offering support are the water and sunlight that help a friendship to grow strong.
- The roots of a plant provide stability. The shared experiences, trust and understanding that grows in a friendship creates a strong foundation.

- With the right care, plants grow and bloom and become beautiful. Similarly, friendships that are nurtured and cared for become strong, meaningful connections that bring joy to everyone involved.
- A garden needs to be weeded regularly to maintain its beauty. In a friendship, there may be misunderstandings or disagreements that need to be resolved in order to stay strong.
- Sometimes, for a variety of reasons, seeds and plants do not grow or they die. Not every friendship will be a long-term one. Sometimes people are friends just for a short time at a particular period in their lives. Sometimes people find out that they are not compatible.

> **Bonus idea** ★
>
> As the plants grow, plant them in a garden or a planter in the school grounds and name this the Friendship Garden. Decorate the garden with stones containing positive friendship messages.

IDEA 62

Family drawing relay

'I liked seeing all the different families.'

This activity gives children the opportunity to see a range of different ideas about what being a family means.

Teaching tip

Emphasise teamwork and cooperation, encouraging all team members to contribute.

Taking it further

Encourage children to be creative by adding family members, pets, activities or anything that represents a family.

Divide the class into groups of four to six children. Give each team a large sheet of paper and a set of drawing materials.

Explain to the children that they will be working together in their teams to create a drawing of a family. Each team member will have a limited time to add one element to the drawing.

Provide the first team member in each group with the drawing materials. Start a timer (adjust the time according to the age of the children, e.g. one to two minutes per turn). The first team member begins by drawing a basic element of a family scene, such as a house or the outline of family members. Once the time is up, they pass the drawing to the next team member, who adds another element.

Continue passing the drawing between group members for a set amount of time, e.g. 20 minutes. When the time is up, ask each group to share their completed family scene and talk through why they chose particular elements.

Use the questions in the discussion:

- What are the similarities and differences between the families? Why is this?
- What makes a family?
- Why are families important?
- What sorts of things do families do together and how do they support one another?

Conclude that all families are different; there is no one way to be a family. What is most important is that all the members of the family care for one another.

IDEA 63

Qualities of healthy friendships

'I think the most important thing is honesty; Noah thinks it is sharing.'

This activity allows children to share their own values and ideas, while also appreciating those of others.

Split the class into small groups. Give each group a set of cards featuring nine friendship qualities, such as honesty, sharing, kindness, listening, respect, communication, trust, boundaries, forgiveness.

Ensure that children have a clear understanding of each, and encourage the class to think of examples. Next, ask the children to work in small groups to discuss and determine which qualities they believe are most important for creating great friendships. Following their discussion, ask each group to sort their cards from least to most important in a diamond shape (i.e. one at the top, two in the next row, three in the middle, and so on).

Once all groups have completed their Diamond Nine, take feedback from the groups using questioning to deepen thinking.

- What are the similarities and differences between the groups? Why is this?
- Was it easy or hard to decide on your Diamond Nine? Why?
- Why might someone value… over… ?
- What would happen if these qualities were not present in a friendship?
- How are these qualities developed?
- Can you give me an example of when you have demonstrated one of these qualities?
- Are there any qualities that you think are important to all types of relationships, and not just friendships?

Teaching tip

If children are not familiar with doing Diamond Nine activities, create a visual on the board to help them to prioritise their cards.

Taking it further

Develop small-group role-plays demonstrating the friendship qualities.

IDEA 64

Quotes

'I love starting an RSE lesson with a quote, getting the children to think about what it means and how it relates to relationships.'

Quotes are a great stimulus for discussions and exploration around healthy relationships and values. They can be used as a starter for a whole class or as a more in-depth group-work activity.

Teaching tip

Remind children that everyone is unique and will have different values and opinions about relationships.

Taking it further

Ask children to create their own quotes about relationships. Display these in the classroom.

Choose quotes that align with the topic that you are covering and the age of the children. Quotes from people or characters that they know will be easier to relate to – for example, quotes from children's films, popstars, sports people or celebrities.

Share the quote with the class and ask them to discuss what it means with their talk-partner. Take feedback and link it to the theme of the lesson. Use questioning to deepen the learning.

Alternatively, split the class into groups and give each group a different quote. Ask them to discuss and then present their views to the rest of the class.

Here is an example of a quote from Winnie the Pooh that could be used to explore love, loss and change: 'You may be gone from my sight. But you are never gone from my heart.' (Winnie the Pooh)

Here are some sample questions to explore the quote:

- What does it mean to have someone in your heart?
- What is love?
- How does it feel when someone is apart from a person or people that they love?
- How would it feel for someone to lose a person or a thing that they love?
- What could help them to deal with this loss?

IDEA 65

Anti-bullying photo exhibition

'The photographs were so varied; they captured the theme in so many different ways.'

Host an anti-bullying photo exhibition to showcase children's ideas about being kind, having healthy relationships and standing up to bullying.

Start the activity with a discussion around bullying: what it is, who can help and the role of bystanders. Ask children what people can do to prevent bullying, and outline the term 'upstander' as someone who actively does something when they witness a bullying situation. Reinforce your school policy on bullying and reporting procedures.

Choose a theme for the anti-bullying photo exhibition – for example, 'Our school says "no" to bullying!', 'Kindness in action' or 'We are upstanders'.

In groups, ask children to plan the photos that they would like to include to illustrate the theme. These could be inside or outside of school and involve people, objects or places. They can be abstract or realistic. Encourage creativity – for example, some children may want to plan and photograph still images (see Idea 43), while others may want to photograph areas of the school, like a buddy bench.

Children take their photographs using a camera or tablet. Edit them as required on the computer. As a whole class, plan how the different photos will be displayed in the school hall or other suitable space. Print the photos on photo paper and mount them. Children can add a header, captions and other decorative items to the exhibition.

Teaching tip

Once the exhibition is over, create a scrapbook with the photographs as a lasting reminder.

Bonus idea ★

Hold an event to share the photographs with the rest of the school, parents and the wider community. Encourage children to talk through their photographs and the messages behind them. Ask visitors to share their thoughts on the exhibition by writing in a visitors' book or making a pledge for how they will be an upstander when they witness bullying.

IDEA 66

Emotional dominoes

'The children had so much fun with this activity and it provoked some great discussion.'

This 'emotional dominoes' activity supports children to explore the impact of relationships on emotions, and how one person's emotions can impact others in a chain reaction.

Teaching tip

Remind children not to use scenarios that are based on real-life incidents in school. You could prepare short scenarios if you want to ensure a variety of scenarios and to save time.

Gather paper, markers and a large open space.

Discuss the concept of a person's emotions impacting on their relationships. Ask whether the children can think of any examples. Explain that our feelings can be influenced by the people around us and that our emotions can also affect others.

In groups, give children five minutes to come up with a list of different emotions. Take responses from the groups, writing each suggested emotion in large writing on a separate piece of A4 paper. If needed, prompt a wide range of emotions, such as happiness, sadness, anger, excitement and so on.

Present a scenario related to relationships – for example, 'Saima shared her ruler with Will.' Ask the children to choose which emotion Will would feel in this situation. Place that 'domino' card on the floor. What would Will do next? Perhaps he might say 'thank you for being kind' to Saima. How does this make Saima feel? Place an appropriate emotion card next to the first one, which has been 'knocked over' as if in a domino rally. Follow the scenario through to a conclusion. Discuss the domino effect of emotions: how one person's actions or feelings can have a knock-on effect on others, like in a domino rally.

In groups, ask children to come up with their own scenario including different interactions between people, both positive and negative. For instance:

- Marcus asked his friend to play computer games but his friend said no.
- Ellie didn't invite Cayla to her sleepover.

Encourage the groups to use their scenario to create their own emotional domino rally. Share each group's ideas.

Use questions to explore the scenarios:

- How did emotions change as they moved through the scenario?
- What did you learn about how relationships can affect emotions?

Finish by reflecting on the impact of relationships on emotions and vice versa. Highlight the importance of kindness, empathy and understanding in our relationships with others, as our actions can have a ripple effect on their feelings.

Taking it further

Work the scenarios into short role-plays.

IDEA 67

Wedding speeches

'Archie is really special to me – he is always supportive and kind.'

Through creating wedding speeches, children learn what is important in a healthy relationship and why people choose to commit through marriage, while also developing their oracy skills.

Teaching tip

Encourage respectful listening during the speeches. Reinforce with children the skills that they have used in the activity, such as group work, planning, speaking and expressing themselves.

Taking it further

Discuss the speeches with the children using these questions as a guide:

- What were the similarities and differences between the speeches?
- Why did these couples decide to get married?
- Do you think that marriage is important?
- Why or why not?
- What are the best reasons for two people to get married?
- What are some poor reasons for two people to get married?

Begin by developing a common understanding of what marriage is, and explaining that in this country the law says that two women, two men or a man and a woman can get married. Ask the children why two people might choose to commit to each other in this way. Discuss what happens at weddings, building in some key information such as preparations, exchanging rings, vows, how weddings are celebrated in different faiths, celebrations, food, wedding cakes and speeches.

In groups, give children ten minutes to create a couple who are going to get married. Encourage them to develop a back-story for their couple. (With younger children, you could choose two toys who are going to get married.)

Explain that usually a key part of weddings in this country is the speeches, where people involved in the wedding, such as those getting married or their relatives, talk about the couple and their relationship. Ask each group to create a speech for both people in their couple to give at the wedding. Encourage them to include in the speech feelings about each other, memories and why they want to commit to each other.

In turn, ask each group to give a little bit of information about their couple and then 'perform' their speeches.

IDEA 68

Relationship snapshots

'In the modern world, we know that many children will be forming relationships online. It's important that we help them to recognise and assess risks.'

This activity highlights the differences between online and face-to-face interactions and the strengths and limitations of both.

Begin by discussing with the children the various ways in which people interact and form relationships.

In groups, ask the children to create two 'relationships snapshots', one representing a face-to-face interaction and the other an online interaction. They can use paper, markers and magazines or printed images to create their snapshot, using collage, drawing and writing. For the face-to-face snapshot, encourage them to create a scene where people are interacting in person, e.g. friends playing together. For the online snapshot, the scene should represent an interaction that happens through a device, e.g. playing a game online.

Once all groups have finished, ask them to present their 'snapshots' to the class. Discuss the differences between the two types of interaction, using the following questions as a guide:

- What's different about the way in which people communicate in these two snapshots?
- How do people express emotions or understand feelings in each?
- What are the advantages and disadvantages of each type of interaction?
- What are the risks associated with online relationships?

Discuss the strengths and limitations of both types of interactions and highlight the significance of maintaining balance and safety in both online and face-to-face relationships.

Teaching tip

Highlight differences between face-to-face interactions (talking in person, body language, tone of voice) and online relationships (chatting, emojis, written communication). Use a video clip showing the two types of interaction to help children get started.

Taking it further

Create a display featuring the 'snapshots' plus some key points from the discussion, including safety rules for online interactions.

Bonus idea ★

Explore how electronic communications can impact face-to-face relationships – for example, text messages can often be misinterpreted because people don't have the benefit of tone and body language.

IDEA 69

Safety detectives

'This activity gave us an opportunity to reinforce school rules and reporting procedures.'

This activity helps children to recognise signs of abusive behaviour and encourages reporting to adults.

Teaching tip

Be ready to offer support to any groups or individuals that find the task difficult. Reinforce that reporting abusive behaviour is not 'telling tales'; it is a crucial step in keeping everyone safe.

Before the session, prepare scenario cards with different situations that depict potentially abusive behaviours relevant to the age of the children in your class. Some examples are:

- During a game, a classmate keeps pushing another child, even after they say stop. The child being pushed looks uncomfortable and tries to move away, but the pushing continues.
- A group of children are laughing at another child and calling them hurtful names because they're not as good at a game that they're playing together.
- A classmate often threatens to end their friendship if another child doesn't do what they say.
- A child receives mean and threatening messages from an anonymous account on a social media platform, making them feel scared and anxious.
- A child tells their friend to keep a secret about something that's hurting them or makes them feel uncomfortable, saying that they'll get in trouble if they tell anyone.
- A child notices that a classmate is always on their own and doesn't play or talk with others. They also see another child making rules for this classmate and not letting them interact freely with others.

Discuss the concept of safety and how it's important to look out for ourselves and others. Explain that, sometimes, certain behaviours can make us feel uncomfortable or unsafe.

In groups, ask children to brainstorm behaviours or actions that could be considered unsafe, unkind or abusive. Encourage them to think about various types of behaviour, including physical, emotional, verbal and digital forms of abuse.

Distribute the scenario cards among the groups. Ask the children to analyse the scenario that they received. Encourage them to identify the behaviours or actions that could be considered abusive. Ask them to also think about what they would do if they experienced or witnessed such behaviour.

Discuss the importance of reporting abusive behaviour to trusted adults. Explain the steps that they should take in or out of school if they ever witness or experience such behaviours, emphasising that reporting helps to keep everyone safe.

Bring the class back together for a discussion. Ask each group to feed back on their scenario, what behaviours they identified and what they would do.

Taking it further

Children could role-play scenarios in groups, focusing on how they would react, assert boundaries and report the behaviour to a trusted adult.

Part 9

Puberty

IDEA 70

What to teach and when

'Children have managed the content around puberty well.'

Teaching around puberty should begin before onset, so that children are prepared for the physical and emotional changes.

Here is an example progression of learning around puberty across different year groups.

- **Reception:** hygiene and handwashing; understanding feelings
- **Year 1:** biological differences between boys and girls, including naming genitals; privacy; ways to keep the body clean
- **Year 2:** life cycles; the needs of people at different ages; how the body grows and changes externally
- **Year 3:** keeping the body clean; simple explanation of hormones and how they change the body; healthy lifestyle choices, including eating, moving and sleeping
- **Year 4:** introduction to the physical and emotional changes of puberty; recap on hormones; why puberty happens; hygiene products and how they are used
- **Year 5:** more detailed information on the physical and emotional changes, including the menstrual cycle and reproductive organs; the range of period products; the role of hormones; how to manage the emotional changes; support systems; respect and empathy for others
- **Year 6:** recap on puberty information from Year 5, including wet dreams, onset of attraction/sexual feelings and masturbation (see Idea 79); real-life examples; body image and the influence of social media; difference between mood swings and mental illness; coping strategies.

Teaching tip

What you deliver and when should be based on the needs of your children.

Bonus idea ★

Share information with parents about your puberty education, so they can support at home. Raise funds through your parent–teacher group to purchase a book about puberty for each child. Consult with parents on a suitable book.

IDEA 71

Continuum of normal

'How do you know whether what's happening to you is normal?'

Use this simple concept to reassure children that there are a variety of ways in which people experience puberty.

During puberty education, I feel that it is important to move children away from the idea that everyone experiences things in the same way. Inevitably, children will talk about the changes that are happening to them; they will observe others and make comparisons. This can lead to feelings of worry, doubt or shame if they feel that they are different to others.

Reinforcing the fact that there is a continuum of what is normal emphasises that puberty is a process of development, and that changes occur at different times and rates for everyone. The goal is to normalise these variations and the idea that differences in physical, emotional and social changes are typical and natural. Here are some examples to show how I use this in my practice:

- When discussing hair growth, I mention that hair grows differently for everyone. One woman might have a neat triangle of hair on her vulva, whereas another might have hair that extends to her upper inner thighs. Some men have lots of hairs on their chest; others have none at all. Some women have hairs around their nipples; others don't.
- With periods, I reflect differences in flow, length and symptoms, as well as the products that women choose to use to manage their periods.
- I talk about the range of breast shapes and sizes and how this can alter through life. This can also be applied to body and penis shapes and sizes.

Teaching tip

Children often want a black-and-white answer to questions and concerns; however, it is important to reflect that, with puberty, there are shades of grey. While most people will experience the same changes, they will experience them in different ways.

Taking it further

Reinforce that while there is a range of things that are considered normal, if a child feels that something is wrong, they are not quite sure or they want more support, they should talk with a trusted adult.

IDEA 72

Anatomy

'The children behaved very maturely and were genuinely interested in learning more.'

Having an understanding of the reproductive organs supports children when learning about the changes of puberty and how babies are made.

Teaching tip

Return to the diagrams and descriptions as needed when describing more complex processes such as menstruation.

When working with children around puberty, use simple diagrams of the internal reproductive organs and genitals as a guide to explain where these parts are in the body and how they work. The following straightforward definitions will help you to describe these parts.

Male reproductive organs and genitals:

- **Testicles:** Two egg-shaped organs that hang behind the penis. They are in a bag or sack called the scrotum. After puberty, the testicles begin to produce sperm. Sperm are cells that can join with an egg to make a baby.
- **Vasa Deferentia:** Tubes that transport the sperm from the testicles to the outside of the body through the penis.
- **Prostate gland:** This produces fluid that mixes with the sperm from the testicles to produce semen. Semen is the fluid that carries the sperm.
- **Urethra:** A tube that runs through the penis, which carries both wee and sperm out of the body.
- **Penis:** An organ in front of the testicles that allows wee and sperm to come out of the body. The penis has a tube of skin over it called the foreskin, which covers the head of the penis. In some people, the top part of the foreskin is removed for religious or health reasons.

Female reproductive organs and genitals:

- **Ovaries:** Two small sacs (ovaries) that produce eggs. The egg cells are in the female body from birth. They begin to develop and be released as the person goes through puberty.
- **Fallopian tubes:** Once a month, an egg travels from one of the ovaries down the fallopian tube towards the womb. If the egg is fertilised by a sperm in the fallopian tube, a baby may grow and develop.
- **Uterus:** This is also known as the womb. It is where a fertilised egg can implant and develop into a baby during pregnancy. If an egg is not fertilised, the lining of the womb is not needed, and it comes out through the vagina. This is a period.
- **Cervix:** A narrow opening that leads from the bottom of the uterus to the vagina. During birth, the cervix gets wider to allow the baby to come out through the vagina.
- **Vagina:** A stretchy muscular tube that leads from the cervix to the outside of the body between the legs.
- **Urethra:** A narrow opening above the vagina where wee comes out.
- **Clitoris:** A small pea-sized bump above the urethra that is a very sensitive part of the female body.

> **Taking it further**
>
> In the following years, use unlabelled diagrams to see whether children remember the names of the different parts.

IDEA 73

Puberty comic strips

'I didn't realise there were so many changes!'

In this activity, children create comic strips to reflect on the physical and emotional changes of puberty.

Teaching tip

Depending on the age and maturity of the class, you may want to select which changes you would like them to illustrate.

Explain to the children that they will be creating a comic strip that shows the physical and emotional changes during puberty.

Ask children to share what they know already about the physical and emotional changes of puberty. Write these up on the board under the headings 'Physical' and 'Emotional'. Share and explain any changes that have not yet been mentioned, using the list below:

Physical changes:

- growth spurts
- development of breasts
- body hair growth (facial hair, pubic hair, leg hair, underarm hair)
- menstruation
- voice changes (deeper voice for boys)
- acne and oily skin
- hair gets greasy
- muscle growth
- increased sweating and body odour
- hips get wider
- penis and testicles grow
- wet dreams
- sperm starts to be produced
- ovaries develop and release eggs
- erections may become more frequent
- discharge comes out of the vagina.

Emotional changes:

- mood swings
- increased sensitivity to emotions
- romantic feelings develop
- increased independence and desire for privacy
- more intense or changing friendships
- feeling self-conscious about physical changes.

Divide the class into pairs or small groups and provide each with a comic strip template. Instruct them to select a physical or emotional change associated with puberty and to create a short story illustrating this change using the comic strip.

Once the comic strips are complete, ask groups to share their creations with the rest of the class. Encourage discussion with questioning:

- Which change did you illustrate?
- Were some easier to illustrate than others? Why?
- How did you represent physical and emotional changes?
- How do people manage the changes of puberty?
- What would support someone going through puberty?
- How can you support others who are going through puberty?

During the discussion, explain that these changes do not happen all at once; they occur gradually over a number of years.

Display the comic strips in the classroom as a reminder for everyone. They could be displayed alongside products that support people to manage puberty, e.g. deodorant, period pads, shower gel, etc.

> **Taking it further**
>
> Ask children to develop and act out some role-plays from the puberty comic strips. Reinforce the group agreement to ensure a safe learning environment. Using role-play encourages discussion about the puberty experiences and develops the children's empathy.

IDEA 74

Puberty bag

'The children said it was their favourite part of the series of lessons. They loved discussing the packaging too and grouping them into who they thought the products were targeted towards.'

Of all the resources to have for RSE, the puberty bag is arguably the cheapest and most versatile. This easy-to-assemble resource can be used to support learning about body hygiene during puberty and beyond.

Teaching tip

Use the discussion around the puberty bag to explore stereotypes and social norms. For example, you might open a discussion about social norms around shaving. Ensure that products used are empty and/or sealed to safeguard pupils.

Gather empty shower gel, shampoo and anti-perspirant/deodorant containers. Sanitise them and place them in a large bag or box. Purchase (or ask for donations of) additional items – for example, soap, toothbrushes and toothpaste, hair-removal items, spot treatment, hairbrushes, body sprays, period products (disposable and reusable pads, period pants, cups, tampons), briefs and boxers, bras, jockstraps, vitamins, make-up, face masks and tweezers. Ensure that your products are inclusive – for example, include a range of hairbrushes and combs for different hair types.

How you use your puberty bag will vary from year group to year group. An idea suitable for use in Year 4 is a simple clue game. Lay all the products out on a table and give children ample time to look over them. Read out some clues to the products and ask pupils in groups to identify which product you are talking about. For example, 'I come in lots of different scents. I can be put onto the skin in different ways. I am used to stop sweat.' You could make it competitive by keeping a tally of points. As each product is identified, lead a discussion about usage and how it supports people to manage puberty changes.

Other ways in which to use your puberty bag include:

- Match the items to the puberty changes that they support.
- Carry out cost comparisons – branded vs supermarket own-brand.
- Explore gender stereotypes through products marketed towards women and men, e.g. shaving foam comes in pink cans for women and blue cans for men.
- Sort the products – essential/non-essential, disposable/reusable, etc.
- Carry out demonstrations, e.g. period pads.
- What would you take to a desert island?
- Design a new puberty product.
- Investigate environmentally friendly options.
- Explore personal preference with regard to products, e.g. shaving.
- Look at adverts for the products – how do they encourage people to buy them? How do they feel about this?

Taking it further

As a follow-up, ask the children to create adverts using the products (see Idea 76).

IDEA 75

Problem texts

'It's OK, you are just having a period. It happens to all girls at a certain point. Just talk to your mum and get some pads.'

Responding to problems from other children is a great way for children to apply their learning, empathise with others and get their own questions answered.

Write some scenarios relating to puberty that children may have problems with or concerns about. Some examples include: not knowing when periods will start, wondering whether to shave or not, being taller than everyone else, feeling embarrassed about the changes they are experiencing and finding it difficult to cope with mood swings.

Type the problems onto a phone template (download it from the internet), cut each one out and laminate it. I find there is added value in children having an individual 'phone' to hold.

Working individually, in pairs or in small groups, give each a 'phone' and ask them to write a response to the child. Encourage children to empathise with the scenario and identify the best advice. They can write on the phone in whiteboard marker.

Take feedback on each 'problem'. Reinforce some key learning points, such as:

- Puberty happens at different times for different people.
- There is a continuum of what is 'normal' in puberty.
- If someone is worried, they can seek help from a parent or another trusted adult.
- Puberty is normal and natural.
- People have different ways of managing puberty changes.
- Personal choice is important.

Teaching tip
This activity can also be used as a pre- or post-assessment opportunity.

Taking it further
Develop the responses into role-plays. Get children to research support agencies that could help the children in the scenarios.

Bonus idea ★
As an alternative, ask children to write some problems that they feel children might face.

IDEA 76

Adverts

'Are we going to do those adverts again?'

In this fun activity, children create adverts to share their learning about hygiene during puberty and beyond.

This is an excellent activity to consolidate learning about puberty hygiene. It is ideal for pupils in Year 4, as they build on their knowledge of puberty. Following input on the physical and emotional changes of puberty, use the puberty bag (see Idea 74) to explore hygiene with the class. Reveal items from the bag one by one. Ask children to identify what the product is, how it is used and what change of puberty it relates to. Ask: 'Why is it important for people to take care of their hygiene during puberty?' Explain that in this time of change and beyond, children need to take more care to keep their bodies clean, so that they do not smell unpleasant or get infections.

Split the class into small groups. Allocate one puberty item to each group. (If you have lots of products, you could let groups choose an item they feel most comfortable with.) Ask the groups to create a television advert featuring their product. In their advert, they must explain what the product is, how it works, the change of puberty that it relates to and what the benefits are to the viewer.

Once all groups have created their advert, share them to the whole class. Ask children to share constructive feedback about the adverts. When all the adverts have been shown, encourage children to reflect on what they have learned and the skills they used in the activity.

Teaching tip

Encourage pupils to think carefully about the content of their advert. The people watching need to learn about the changes of puberty that this product relates to, how it is used and the benefits. Use the development time to observe and listen to pupils, picking up on any misconceptions or gaps in knowledge. Record or photograph the adverts and share via a QR code in your floorbook (see Idea 97) or on your class sharing platform, e.g. Seesaw.

Taking it further

Ask each group to research their hygiene item further, identifying different brands and price points. Encourage groups to identify whether there are eco-friendly alternatives and why this is important.

IDEA 77

Puberty bingo

'Is it a line or a full house?'

Puberty bingo is a fun way to engage children with their learning around puberty changes. This is an activity that can be adapted for use in all year groups in Key Stage 2.

Teaching tip

When the first people shout 'puberty', point out that, just as in life, they and their friends will reach puberty at different ages. As an alternative to puberty changes bingo, particularly if they are feeling uncomfortable, try adding puberty hygiene items or puberty worries to the cards.

Prepare a bingo card for each child in the class, featuring the physical and emotional changes of puberty. Ideally, there will be a variety of different cards so that not every child will complete their card at the same time. You will also need a set of cards with the puberty changes to draw out of a bag.

Draw out the changes one at a time and ask the children to cross each off on their sheet. Use questions to check understanding of each change: What is this change? Why does it happen? Is this a change for boys, girls or both? How could someone manage this change?

The first child (or children) to cross off their whole card shouts, 'Puberty!'

Here are some sample changes (choose ones that are suitable for the age group with which you are working):

- Breasts develop.
- Hair grows on the face.
- Feelings of attraction may develop.
- Hair grows under the arms.
- Sperm starts to be produced.
- Hair grows on the legs.
- Hair gets greasy.
- Ovaries develop and release eggs.
- Body produces more oil and sweat.
- Body grows taller.
- Shoulders and chest get broader.
- Periods start.
- May have erections.

- Voice gets deeper.
- May have wet dreams.
- Moods change a lot.
- Discharge comes out of the vagina.
- Pubic hair grows around the genitals.
- Penis and testicles get bigger.

Some information to support the discussion includes:

- Puberty happens so that when a person is older, they can make a baby if they choose to.
- The release of hormones begins the process of puberty.
- Puberty happens to people at different times: the average age to begin puberty is eight to 12 for girls and ten to 14 for boys.
- Puberty lasts for about four to five years.
- There are a range of things that are 'normal' in puberty. Not everyone experiences it in the same way. If someone is worried about any of the changes, they can talk to a trusted adult.

Teaching tip

Use puberty bingo as an icebreaker at the beginning of your lessons on puberty. Encourage children to reflect on their feelings about the phrases on the bingo card as they play, creating an open dialogue to address any questions or concerns that arise.

IDEA 78

Menstruation

'We felt that it was important to reduce the stigma around menstruation by getting the whole class involved in activities.'

Children understanding the process of menstruation is one part of learning in RSE; reducing the stigma around periods and encouraging open conversations is equally important. These activities delve deeper into period products and management.

Teaching tip

If your budget doesn't stretch to buying the actual products, take screenshots to share with the class.

Taking it further

Pose the question: 'Why is it important for boys to learn about periods?' I find that boys always come up with great reasons why, such as if they have a daughter in the future or if they have a female partner. Posing this question gives them a reason to engage with the session.

Bonus idea ★

Explore how people managed menstruation through history; there are lots of images and information online. Compare this to how periods are managed today.

Period products

There are a wealth of products to manage periods, both disposable and reusable. Create a set of products to show children, including disposable pads and tampons, washable period pants, washable pads, period cups, reusable tampon applicators, period sportswear and swimwear. Let the children handle the products to become familiar with them.

Collect products for your local foodbank

Hold a campaign within school to gather period products for a local foodbank. Explain the term 'period poverty' to the children and reinforce to them where they can access these products in school if they need them.

Make reusable pads

Run a sewing project to create reusable pads for the school or to donate. There are lots of videos online demonstrating how to make them. You could enlist the help of your parent teacher group or the local Women's Institute. Enclose a card with each one, showing how to wash and take care of them.

Period-tracking apps

Demonstrate how to use a period-tracking app and how they can help to manage periods. Take screenshots to share with the children.

IDEA 79

Masturbation

'It's all a bit awkward, isn't it? I mean, you don't want to encourage them.'

Including discussion around masturbation in RSE in primary schools requires careful consideration, to ensure that information is age-appropriate and respectful of a range of values and cultural perspectives.

Including the topic of masturbation in RSE should aim to provide accurate and age-appropriate information, while promoting self-awareness, respect for privacy and an understanding that, for some people, this is a natural part of human development. Always maintain a non-judgemental and supportive approach when addressing this topic.

When children are learning about the changes of puberty, this is an ideal time to include reference to masturbation, as it will link with discussion around the onset of sexual feelings and attraction. This is likely to be in the more advanced puberty lessons in the later years of primary. Explain that masturbation is something that some people do to explore their bodies and experience pleasurable sensations. Tell children that families and cultures may have different beliefs and values regarding this topic.

Reinforce the importance of privacy and personal boundaries, explaining that masturbation is something that is done in private, such as in a bathroom or bedroom (as long as the room is not shared).

You may choose to script a sentence, such as: 'Masturbation is when someone touches their genitals because they find it pleasurable. Some people agree with it and some people don't; the most important thing to remember is that it is a private activity.'

Teaching tip

Be prepared for questions; think through how you might answer these. Prepare simple age-appropriate statements to respond.

Bonus idea ★

Involve parents in the conversation by providing them with information on what will be discussed in the classroom. Some children – for example, those with special educational needs – may need a more explicit approach to ensure that they understand the social rules around masturbation; Social Stories™ are useful for this.

Part 10

Sex

IDEA 80

Making the choice to start a family

'There's a lot to think about when people start a family.'

This activity encourages children to consider the various factors involved in making decisions about starting a family and to appreciate the responsibilities of parenthood.

Teaching tip

Be mindful of children's family experiences and offer support to those who need it before and during the lesson.

Taking it further

During the discussion, explore how families come in lots of different variations and can be made in different ways, e.g. through adoption and fostering.

Bonus idea ★

As a class, create a timeline using two of the characters, from meeting and beginning a relationship to starting a family.

Begin the activity with a discussion about families. Ask the children what families mean to them and what makes a family. Introduce the concept of life choices, explaining that people make different decisions in life based on their values, wants and needs. These decisions impact on their future.

Divide the class into small groups or pairs. Ask them to create a character and decide on this character's name, age, occupation, hobbies and dreams. Make one of your own too. Once created, encourage children to discuss whether their character wants to have a family in the future.

As a whole class, discuss the factors that are important in planning a family – for instance, stability, commitment, strong relationships and money. Discuss what each of these means, to check understanding. Using your character, take one factor and discuss how it might affect their choice to start a family.

Ask each group to take one factor and discuss how it might affect their own character's decision to start a family. Present each group's ideas to the class. Encourage discussions and questions.

Conclude the session by reinforcing how important it is for people to consider the various factors before making life-changing decisions like starting a family.

IDEA 81

Family identity boxes

'It was exciting opening the boxes and looking at the stuff inside!'

In this immersive activity, children explore the range of ways in which families are made by examining family identity boxes.

Assemble a variety of family identity boxes using old shoe boxes. Each box should represent a different family formation story or structure. Include photographs, artifacts, letters, objects and/or symbols that embody the essence of each family. These items can be sourced online or created. Prepare enough boxes for each group to have one.

Here are some example contents for a family formed through adoption:

- adoption papers
- storybooks about adoption
- stuffed animals
- photographs and letters from the adoptive parents to the adopted child
- cultural artifacts reflecting the cultural heritage of the child
- brochures or print-outs about adoption.

Start the session by exploring the concept of diverse family structures and understanding the ways in which families come together.

Put the children into groups and give each group a family identity box. Ask them to examine the contents of their box carefully and make some notes on what they find. Encourage them to hypothesise about the family's formation story, based on the items in the box.

Invite each group to share their box and ideas. Discuss the similarities and differences between the family structures. What emotions did they feel when looking at the box? What is important in this family?

Teaching tip

Different family structures that could be represented include: blended or stepfamilies, extended families, single-parent families, foster families, adoptive families, same-sex families, childless families, grandparent families, families separated by geography through work or migration and co-parenting families.

Taking it further

Make the contents of the boxes sturdy so that they can be reused time and again.

Bonus idea ★

Discuss with the children what they discovered about how families are made. Emphasise the importance of empathy, respect and appreciation of the diverse ways in which families are formed.

117

IDEA 82

Reproduction

'My mum said you buy the baby at the shop.'

Exploring reproduction with children in a safe and supportive environment helps to prepare them for more in-depth work around sex and sexual health at secondary school. Here are some tips on how to explain reproduction to primary-age children.

Teaching tip

Use appropriate visual aids to explain the process of reproduction, such as diagrams or short videos or animations. I often use a video of an embryo growing in the womb that I sourced on YouTube and an animation of birth.

When exploring reproduction, use simple explanations appropriate to the age of the children. For example:

'Human reproduction is how babies are made. Sometimes, two people who love each other and want to have a baby decide to start a family. When they're ready, a special cell from a female body, called an egg, meets a special cell from a male body, called sperm. These cells come together inside the female body, and that's how a baby starts to grow. The baby grows inside the body for about nine months until it's ready to be born. Then, the baby comes into the world and brings a lot of joy and happiness to the people who are going to take care of it.'

As children get older, more can be added about the process of sexual intercourse:

'The egg and the sperm usually come together when two people have sexual intercourse, which is when a man's penis goes into a woman's vagina. During sexual intercourse, the man's sperm travels to meet the woman's egg in the fallopian tube. The sperm joins with the egg and travels to the woman's womb, where it grows into a baby. This growth takes about nine months, and during this time, the baby gets everything it needs from the mother's body. When the baby is fully grown and ready, it's born through the vagina or via a cut made in the mum's tummy.'

Here are some tips:

- Put the learning in context by introducing the concept of reproduction using examples from nature, such as plants or animals.
- Make links to puberty education, explaining that puberty is preparing the body to be able to reproduce.
- Emphasise that reproduction is a natural part of life and growth for many living things, including humans.
- For younger children, use age-appropriate picture books or stories that illustrate the reproductive process or the growth of the baby.
- With older children, talk about the different ways in which the sperm and egg can come together – for example, through in-vitro fertilisation (IVF) or sperm or egg donation.

> **Taking it further**
>
> When discussing reproduction, be mindful of the diverse family structures of the children in your class. Acknowledge that there are many different family types, including single-parent, same-sex parents, and extended families. Use inclusive language and examples that reflect this diversity, ensuring that every child feels represented and valued.

IDEA 83

Sensory stations

'It's difficult to know how to talk about pleasure, but it is important.'

This activity introduces the concept of pleasure in an age-appropriate way using sensory stations, laying the foundation for future discussions as children get older.

Set up sensory stations in the classroom, each focusing on a different sense:

- **Tactile station:** Include a range of tactile experiences – for instance, soft fabrics, squishy balls, smooth stones, sandpaper, slime, clay and cotton wool. Encourage children to explore and describe how these items feel against their skin.
- **Scent station:** Gather scented items such as flowers, essential oils, herbs and scented candles. Ask children to smell them and discuss which scents they find pleasant or soothing.
- **Visual station:** Display a range of pictures, visually appealing objects, vibrant materials, black-and-white images, magazine clippings and colours. Encourage children to discuss which visuals they find attractive, interesting or calming.
- **Auditory station:** Include a range of music and sounds – for instance, pop music, nature sounds, whistles, horns and percussion instruments. Hold a discussion about how different sounds make them feel – relaxed, happy or excited.

Rotate the children through each station, allowing time for them to explore and experience the sensations at each one. Tell them that there is absolutely no obligation for them to touch, smell, look at or listen to anything that they don't like.

Teaching tip

As children make their way around the stations, reinforce messages around consent; empower them to make their own choices about which sensations they want to engage in.

Once all children have experienced each station, have a class discussion about their experiences. Encourage them to express which sensations they found most pleasing or enjoyable and which they didn't enjoy.

Ask the children: What do you notice as people are giving feedback? Did everyone feel the same about the different sensations? Why? Reinforce that we all like different things and that is OK. It is OK to express what we like and don't like, even if it is different to others.

With older children, this activity could link into learning about sex, reproduction and pleasure. For example, you could say something like: 'Much like the way we've explored different sensations and experiences through our senses, as individuals grow into adults and have romantic, intimate relationships, they will communicate with each other about what types of touch they enjoy and don't enjoy. This is part of consent – being able to say yes or no to different sensations.'

Taking it further

Provide children with a simple tick-list or scale to note down their comfort levels with different sensations. Use these to guide the discussion following the activity. Ask children to personally reflect on what sensations they like and don't like before discussing as a whole group. Reinforce that it is okay for people to like different things, and that these preferences should be respected by others.

IDEA 84

Sexual consent

'This activity helped the class to understand consent and the feelings associated with it.'

Discussion around sexual consent should build on prior learning around body safety and boundaries in earlier years. This permission-seeking activity puts consent into context for the children. It is designed to form part of lessons around sex and reproduction in later primary.

Teaching tip

Ensure that everyone feels safe in the activity by reinforcing the group agreement at the beginning of the lesson.

Ask the children what they understand by the term 'consent' and work towards a definition – for example, consent is when two people agree to do something together and feel happy about it.

Explain that when it comes to sexual activity, there are laws by which people must abide. Ask whether anyone knows about these laws. Use the following statement to clarify: The law says that people must be 16 or over to consent to sex.

Tell the children that they are going to play a game of 'consent pass' to illustrate how consent works and how it feels. Choose a soft toy or ball. Emphasise that this game is about asking for, giving and receiving consent.

Give the object to one child. Explain that the person holding the object will ask someone else in the class, 'Can I pass this to you?' The child being asked for consent can respond with a 'yes' or 'no'. If they say 'yes', the child can pass it to them; if they say 'no', they must respect the decision and not pass it to that child. Continue the game, encouraging the children to use positive reinforcement when consent is asked for and given: 'Thank you for asking' or 'I appreciate you for respecting my choice.'

After the game, use the questions below to explore feelings:

- How did it feel when someone asked for consent before passing the object?
- How did it feel when someone said 'yes'/'no'?
- How did it feel when someone respected your decision?
- Why is consent important?

In the discussion, reinforce some key rules around consent, relating these to both the current activity and to sexual activity:

- Just because someone says 'yes' to something one time, that does not mean that they will or have to say 'yes' another time.
- People should not put pressure on others to consent; they must accept their decision.
- People can change their mind at any time, and this must be respected.

Taking it further

Based on the learning from this activity, involve children in creating 'Consent Conversation Cards', featuring sentences they can use to assert their rights around consent and accept others' choices. For instance, they might use sentences like, 'I feel uncomfortable about that' or 'I respect your decision'. Use these cards in role-play, to support discussion around consent scenarios, or have them on a display in the classroom.

IDEA 85

Contraception

'It's like the skin on a sausage.'

Sensitive discussion around contraception can form part of broader coverage of sex and reproduction in later primary years.

Teaching tip

In my experience, some children will already have basic knowledge about contraception by late primary school. Whether or not to include exploration of contraception is a decision for your school, to be informed by your context and pupil voice.

Taking it further

Reflect a range of different perspectives around contraception – for example, 'Some people in some faiths believe that artificial methods of contraception are not appropriate.'

Discuss the concept of planning and making choices in everyday life. Ask children to suggest some examples of plans and choices that they make – for example, what to do at the weekend or what to eat for breakfast.

Ask children what they know or think about how people decide when or whether to have a baby. Introduce the idea that some adults will use methods to plan when to have a baby; these are called forms of 'contraception'. Ask whether anyone has heard of this term before. Explain that all types of contraception can reduce the risk of an unwanted baby being made, and some types also protect people from infections that can be passed on during sex.

Use the whiteboard or large paper to list or draw simple representations of contraception – for example, contraceptive pills or condoms. Explain that contraception works to reduce the risk of unwanted pregnancy by stopping sperm from being able to fertilise an egg. Some types, such as condoms, prevent infections by not allowing body fluids to mix.

Reinforce key messages:

- Sometimes, a man and woman have sex when they don't want to make a baby. They use contraception to reduce the risk of a baby being made.
- There has to be consent for sex to take place. The age of consent is 16.
- Condoms can reduce the risk of infections being passed on during sex.

IDEA 86

Parenting

'When we do lessons on parenting, it helps children to appreciate and empathise with their grown-ups at home.'

These activities help children to explore and understand the responsibilities of being a parent.

Early Primary

Prepare a variety of objects or images related to parenting responsibilities – for instance, oven gloves, washing-up liquid, money, books, toys, passport, hairbrush, etc. In small groups or as a whole class, sort the items into categories such as 'care', 'teach' and 'play'. Discuss the many roles that parents play in a child's life. Ask the children to identify anything that they feel is missing from the items. What do they feel is the most important quality of a parent?

Late Primary

As a whole class, discuss the sorts of tasks that a parent might carry out in a day. Gather lots of different ideas – for instance, getting up, showering, preparing breakfast, taking children to school and going to work. In groups, ask children to create a daily routine chart showing a typical day in a parent's life. Each group presents their routine chart. Lead a discussion about the similarities and differences between the groups. Explore how routines may change based on life circumstances – for example, if a parent or child is poorly.

Teaching tip

Be mindful of any circumstances that may make it difficult for a child to feel safe and comfortable in this lesson.

Questions and challenging issues

Part 11

IDEA 87

Questions, questions, questions

'But how did the baby get in the mummy's tummy?'

Children are curious; they ask lots of questions. It is important that they have this opportunity in RSE to ensure they get the information they need.

I find that responding to children's questions is the area that provokes most anxiety for teachers. This is often due to fear of parents' reactions to how a question is answered. Children should feel free to ask questions, even if they are difficult to answer. There is a need to create an environment where children feel comfortable and confident to ask their questions.

So, how do you answer questions in an effective way? Firstly, know what your school's RSE policy says about answering children's questions. This should guide your responses.

Before answering any questions, consider:

- Is this question relevant to the current lesson? If not, you may want to delay answering until a more appropriate time, or give an individual answer at the end of the lesson.
- What do I know about this child? How old are they? Is this question something that I would expect from a child of this age and/or this particular child?
- Is this something that I will cover later? If the question touches on a topic that is due to be covered later, you could ask the child to hold it until then.

Teaching tip

Be wary of not answering or addressing certain questions, particularly those asked in front of the whole class. If you choose not to answer, children may seek the answers online and be exposed to inappropriate content. Employing the use of a question box (see Idea 88) minimises this possibility.

Some key strategies for answering questions include:

- Develop a group agreement and have a statement around questions (see Idea 27).
- Take a breath and take your time; don't feel the need to answer immediately. Give a holding statement: 'That's a really interesting question. I'm going to return to that later.' Ensure that you do answer later, once you have had the chance to formulate your response.
- Ask for more information: Can you tell me what you know already? I'm wondering where you heard that phrase?
- Consider the key messages (see Idea 41) that you want to impart in answering the question.
- Answer in an honest, factual, non-judgemental way, without any personal opinions.
- Ask the class whether they can help with an answer.

Be mindful of safeguarding concerns arising from questions. If you are worried about a child's questions, log it with your DSL.

Taking it further

Consider scripting answers to questions (see Idea 92)

IDEA 88

Question box

'Well, sometimes they just ask questions to embarrass you, don't they?'

The question box has several purposes in an RSE lesson: it supports staff who feel less confident in answering questions and it gives each child an opportunity to ask the questions that they need to, regardless of how confident they feel. It is suitable for all classes where children can write independently.

Teaching tip

You could introduce a coding system for the questions, so one symbol is used if children want an answer in front of the class and a different one is used if they want a private answer.

Before delivering any RSE to a year group, consider what your rules around questions are; put these in the class group agreement (see Idea 27). Refer back to the rules as needed.

Prepare a question box, using a shoebox, printer paper box or similar. At the start of each RSE lesson, put slips of scrap paper onto each table. Explain to the children that they can write a question at any point during the session and put it into the question box. It is advisable to ask children to write their name on the slip for safeguarding purposes; however, you can reassure them that you won't read their name out.

By collecting questions in this way, it allows you:

- more time to formulate responses
- an opportunity to consult with colleagues
- the option to group questions together – for example, if when delivering sex education, you get lots of questions about sexual practices, you can give a generic answer (see Idea 90)
- to give personal responses to a child on a one-on-one basis if an answer is not deemed relevant for the whole class
- to consider any safeguarding concerns
- to involve parents in supporting a child's understanding of a particular concept.

IDEA 89

Personal questions

'When did you start your periods?'

As a primary teacher, you inevitably develop close relationships with the children in your class, and they will be curious about your life outside of school. While you may share some information about your life with them, this becomes more challenging when teaching sensitive topics within RSE.

To avoid having to answer more sensitive questions in RSE, include in your group agreement (see Idea 27) a rule stating 'no personal questions'. Ensure that children know what a personal question is and why this rule is important. Reinforce that during RSE this is a rule that covers questions to both you and other children in class. While you may feel OK with answering some personal questions, if we allow some, it becomes more challenging to not answer others, so a blanket policy is better.

If a child asks a personal question – let's take the one above as an example – you could simply respond: 'Thank you for your question, but that is a personal question and we agreed that we wouldn't ask and answer those in RSE.'

In order to ensure that the child doesn't feel shamed and gets some response to their question, you might add one of the following to the statement above:

- '... however, I'd really like to ask the class whether they know what the average ages are for girls to start the changes of puberty.'
- '... but we know that people go through puberty at different ages, and when girls start their periods will vary.'
- '... but sometimes girls start their periods at about the same age as their mum started their periods, although not always.'

Teaching tip

Be consistent in sticking to the rules around personal questions, as this supports a safe environment for you and your pupils.

IDEA 90

Explicit questions

'What's a blow job?'

Children may ask explicit questions about sexual practice, based on things that they have heard or seen. Handle these questions with sensitivity, honesty and age-appropriate information.

Teaching tip

Before teaching, brainstorm questions that might be asked by children and consider how you might answer them.

In responding to explicit questions, consider the age-appropriate key messages that you want to give to children around sex – for example, sex should be consensual, sex is for those aged 16 and over. You should use your professional judgement when responding to questions, as well as your school policy.

Consider the age of the child and the context in which explicit questions are asked. If the 'What's a blow job?' question is asked by a young child or outside of an RSE lesson, first ask 'I'm wondering where you have heard that phrase?' so that you can be sure of what it is that the child is asking. They may have heard an older child using it in the park. Also—consider whether the nature of the questions being asked by a child gives rise to any safeguarding concerns.

When I am teaching, I often get questions around sexual practice, and tend to respond in a similar way, using a set phrase that brings in key messages. In response to 'What's a blow job?', I might respond with the following: 'When two adults are in a loving and caring relationship, they may choose to have sex together; this is where they kiss and touch each other in different ways that give them pleasure. There is not just one way to do this, as people like different things. A "blow job" is a slang name for a type of sex. Sex is a private activity for adults, where both people have agreed and feel safe.'

Bonus idea ★

Employ strategies to limit the chance of these questions being asked in front of the whole class, such as a question box (see Idea 88). This gives you time to formulate responses to questions, perhaps in consultation with colleagues.

IDEA 91

Encouraging questions

'There are always those children who don't ask questions but you sense there is something they want to know.'

To support all children to get the answers that they need, use strategies to encourage questions.

Ensure that you have a safe learning environment by creating a group agreement, including a statement around questions. Remind children that there is no such thing as a silly question.

Here are some strategies that you could use to further encourage questions from all children.

At certain points in the lesson, stop and ask all children to write a question on a sticky note or slip of scrap paper. If they can't think of a question, they could write an observation or something that they have learned. This takes away the focus on individuals writing questions and means that only the person asking the question will know that it is theirs.

Individually or in groups, ask the class to think of as many questions as they can that children their age might want to know about the topic. This distancing technique reduces stigma and supports children to ask the questions that they want to ask without it being personal to them. You could ask groups to write their questions or, with younger children, hold a whole-class question-and-answer session.

Present a scenario linked to the topic. Ask children to consider what questions each character in the scenario might have. Again, these can be written down to be answered by the teacher or a whole-class discussion held.

Teaching tip

Give examples of questions so that children have some ideas.

IDEA 92

Scripting

'I've got no idea how to answer this!'

Scripting is a useful way of ensuring consistency across school when answering RSE-related questions from pupils and parents. Having a bank of sample answers to questions for different year groups is helpful, particularly for less confident or new staff.

Teaching tip

You may choose to add some example scripted responses in an appendix to your RSE policy. This will develop parents' understanding of how questions will be answered.

As a staff group, brainstorm questions that children of different ages might ask during RSE lessons, including those that people would find tricky to answer. Challenge everyone to write an answer and then discuss responses, using the following questions as a guide:

- Which answers are best for which year groups?
- Which are most in line with our school values and ethos?
- Do the answers reinforce key messages that we would like to promote in each year group and across school, e.g. the importance of consent?
- Are there any that we wouldn't answer? Why?

Encourage staff to share questions that they have been asked before and how they answered them. On reflection, is there anything that they would change about their answer?

Scripting is a useful way in which to build confidence and offer reassurance to staff who are teaching RSE for the first time. It would, however, be impossible to script an answer to every question. A combination of strategies outlined in this chapter should be employed.

Part 12

Assessment and evidence

IDEA 93

What and why?

'But isn't life the assessment?'

RSE is a school subject, and we need to use assessment to know that children are achieving outcomes and making progress.

Teaching tip

Use your assessment data to plan future lessons and to provide clear feedback to children on how to develop further.

Taking it further

Use a range of assessment types to support your RSE teaching:

- **Diagnostic:** finding out where children are at before beginning a topic or series of lessons
- **Formative:** ongoing through the learning process, allowing you to give children feedback and flex your teaching to meet their needs
- **Summative:** evaluating learning at the end of a topic or series of lessons.

I often hear people objecting to RSE assessment because they liken it to assessing the personality of the child. Fundamentally, in RSE, as with any other subject, you are assessing how well children meet the learning outcomes that you have set. These could be focused on knowledge and understanding, skills development, attitudinal shifts or a combination of all three. If we don't know that children are learning, there seems little point in delivering RSE.

As well as informing you of children's progress, using assessment in RSE also:

- elevates the subject to the same status as others in school
- allows you to share progress in RSE with parents
- highlights children's misconceptions that need addressing
- informs you of individual support needs
- raises a child's awareness of their strengths and areas for development
- enhances self-esteem as children celebrate their achievements
- gives you data to share with leaders.

When assessing RSE, use a range of methods to accommodate different learning styles – for instance, written assessments, interactive discussions, reflective activities, role-play and drawing.

IDEA 94

Draw and Write

'This is not just an assessment method; it's a window into children's thoughts and perspectives.'

This is an accessible and fun method for assessing children's knowledge that can be used with a range of year groups.

The Draw and Write technique is a simple assessment method developed by Noreen Wetton in 1988. It can be used for both formative and summative assessment across a range of RSE topics. The basic premise is that children draw and write their responses to a stimulus. It gives you a snapshot of children's views and knowledge at the start of a topic and can be returned to at the end to demonstrate learning.

Here's an example of how the Draw and Write technique could be used with young children at the start of learning around families. Give each child a piece of paper and a pencil. Read the prompts below and ask children to draw and write their responses.

'Alina is six and she lives with her family.' *Draw Alina's family and add some writing.* 'Alina and her family care for one another a great deal.' *How do they show that they care for one another? Draw and write your ideas.*

Once complete, examine the drawings to identify common themes and patterns. The analysis will inform your upcoming lessons, helping you to tailor your teaching to address the children's perspectives and understanding.

Return the drawings to the children at the end of the topic and ask whether they would make any changes or additions based on their learning. Drawings can be displayed in the children's individual books or in a floorbook (see Idea 97).

Teaching tip

Explain to children that there are no right or wrong ideas, and encourage them to use their own thoughts. If they can't think of anything, that is OK too.

Taking it further

Try using this technique for another area of RSE. For example, before lessons on puberty in Year 4, try: 'Chloe and Tyreece are wondering how their bodies will change as they grow. Draw the changes.'

IDEA 95

Brainstorm

'A really simple and effective way of finding out what children know about a topic.'

Brainstorming is perfect for a snapshot baseline or summative assessment in RSE for children who can write.

Teaching tip

Read through the children's responses to identify any misconceptions or gaps that you can address through the lesson content and delivery.

At the start of a unit of teaching, put a large piece of paper (flip-chart paper would work well) on each table. Give each child in the table group a different-coloured pencil or pen. Ask them to create a key at the top of the sheet with their name and pencil/pen colour.

Pose a question related to your topic and ask children to write down their individual responses on the sheet of paper; these could be individual words or phrases. Give a time limit to encourage children to write their initial thoughts.

Here are some example questions:

Taking it further

You could photograph contributions to add to a floorbook or a child's individual book.

- What makes a happy family?
- What makes a good friend?
- How do you keep safe online?
- What is an unhealthy relationship?
- What changes happen during puberty?

Spend some time receiving feedback from each group.

Following delivery of the unit, return the paper to the groups. In a different coloured pen or pencil, ask children to write new learning and correct any misinformation. Remember to ask children to add to the key with their new pen/pencil colour.

IDEA 96

Role-play

'Role-play isn't just performance; it's assessment in action.'

Role-play provides children with the chance to showcase their skills and understanding. By observing these role-plays, you can gauge the extent to which the children have grasped the learning outcomes.

Role-play is an ideal method with which to assess skills development. RSE skills that can be assessed through role-play include negotiation, conflict resolution, making friends, asking for help, expressing boundaries and consent.

In order for role-play to be valuable as an assessment tool, consider the following:

- Establish which skill you would like children to demonstrate.
- Choose the focus – for example, a scenario or characters from which children can choose.
- Be clear that the role-play is make-believe by giving a start and end signal.
- Encourage children to be authentic and realistic.
- Specify a strict no-physical-contact policy to maintain a safe environment.
- Conclude each role-play with a debrief discussion to reflect on children's experiences.

Here's an example scenario to assess Year 3 children's skills and understanding around consent:

'Sam keeps trying to hold Billy's hand at lunchtime. Billy doesn't like it.'

As children engage in the role-play, circulate with a checklist to mark when you observe the identified skills being demonstrated.

Teaching tip

Manage children's expectations by putting the emphasis on the process of role-playing and not a performance at the end. You may choose to show some excellent examples that you have observed; however, this is not the aim of the activity.

Taking it further

Photograph the role-plays and ask children to annotate the photographs with writing. These can be stuck in individual or class books.

IDEA 97

Floorbooks

'It's great to reflect back with the children on their learning in RSE.'

Floorbooks are a great way in which to capture evidence of children's learning in RSE and demonstrate the RSE journey through a particular year group.

Teaching tip
Use the floorbook in class discussions to remind children of their learning over the term or year.

Taking it further
Display a sample of floorbooks in the reception area or on parents' evenings, so that parents can get a feel for the breadth of RSE.

A floorbook, as its name suggests, is a large blank scrapbook to record learning. It is a collaborative approach between you and the children, with both contributing to demonstrate how learning progresses. The floorbook should be easily accessible to the children and they should be able to contribute to it.

There are lots of ways in which to use a floorbook within RSE; some ideas are given below:

- Stick in pictures of role-play, with children's annotations of what they were saying.
- Have a key question in the centre, with children's responses around the outside, e.g. What makes a family?
- Record new vocabulary learned.
- Include speech bubbles with children's questions or comments related to a particular topic.
- Add photographs of activities – for example, sorting activities like Diamond Nine.

In some schools, I've seen QR codes used within the floorbook to link to audio or video content. This is a great way in which to capture live discussion, role-plays or presentations.

The floorbook is not a way in which to assess individual children's progress; rather, it provides evidence of the class learning journey.

IDEA 98

Quizzes

'Can we do a quiz again?'

Quizzes are a simple way to get a snapshot of children's knowledge and understanding.

There are a range of benefits to using a quiz as an assessment tool in RSE:

- It gives immediate feedback to both you and the children about their strengths and areas for development, allowing you to tailor your teaching.
- Answering questions in the quiz supports the retrieval of information, which is effective for reinforcing learning and promoting long-term retention.
- Quizzes are engaging and many children will enjoy the competitive nature.
- They can be used for both formative and summative assessment.
- They build confidence, as children see their progression over time.

Include a range of questions in your quizzes to provide variety and interest:

- multiple choice
- true/false questions
- fill in the blanks
- matching
- ordering or sequencing.

For more in-depth quizzes used for summative assessment, you could include short scenarios for the children to respond to.

Children can self-mark or peer-mark or the quizzes can be marked by you. If tablets are available, set up a quiz electronically for easy marking.

Teaching tip

Reassure children that the quiz shows their strengths and areas for development and is an opportunity to develop their knowledge and understanding further.

IDEA 99

RAG-rating

'If we are not assessing learning in RSE, how do we know it's working?'

RAG-rating offers a simple visual method for benchmarking pupils and showing progress in RSE.

Assessing knowledge, understanding and skills is a crucial part of RSE. Using 'I can' statements is an effective way in which to set clear expectations for what children should aim for. Once these statements are established, you can use a RAG-rating (red, amber, green) system to assess progress. This assessment approach can be led by you or involve self-assessment or peer-assessment by the children. Self- and peer-assessment are great ways of encouraging reflection and supporting children to take ownership of their learning by identifying strengths and weaknesses.

Working from your scheme or curriculum framework, create specific 'I can' statements that correspond to your learning outcomes. For instance:

- 'I can list some positive friendship qualities.'
- 'I can demonstrate the skills needed to make a friend.'

Set up a grid that includes your 'I can' statements, along with a way of benchmarking each one. For teacher assessment, you can use the RAG system, where:

- Red signifies 'not met' (the child has not achieved the outcome).
- Amber represents 'partially met' (the child has made some progress but hasn't fully achieved the outcome).
- Green indicates 'fully met' (the child has successfully achieved the outcome).

Teaching tip

You could also assess observed behaviours within school, e.g. a child demonstrating kind behaviour on the playground could be highlighted by a lunchtime supervisor.

Taking it further

After the assessments, give feedback to children on their strengths and areas for development. If peer-assessment is being used, spend time beforehand outlining how children can give supportive and constructive feedback.

Bonus idea ★

For child self-assessment or peer-assessment, you could use happy, sad and neutral faces or a set of words, such as disagree/don't know/agree or never/sometimes/always.

IDEA 100

Displays, podcasts, leaflets

'They had so much fun, it didn't seem like assessment at all!'

Assessment doesn't have to be dull; it can be a fun part of the learning. Supporting children to develop displays, podcasts and leaflets allows them to apply their learning in a creative way.

Using these assessment techniques encourages children to reflect on their learning and extract the key learning points to share with others. It gives you, as the teacher, evidence to show the learning.

Displays

Children can contribute to a display to demonstrate their learning about a topic. Examples of topics include healthy friendships, personal space and boundaries, families and anti-bullying. Encourage children to express themselves creatively – for example, through drawing, graphics, poems, scenarios and captions to demonstrate their learning. With older children, you could task them with designing the display.

Podcasts

Children can develop podcasts to showcase their learning. Working in groups, they script their podcast, which could include interviews with classmates and the teacher. Record the podcasts on a tablet to share with other children within school and/or parents.

Leaflets

Children use the knowledge they have learned to create an information leaflet. In groups, they consider their audience, plan the content and write and design the leaflet.

> **Teaching tip**
>
> Ensure that children have clear assessment criteria before they begin the creative process.

> **Teaching tip**
>
> Using the methods on this page not only assesses children's learning but also promotes active engagement and understanding of age-appropriate RSE concepts. The methods allow children to express themselves and develop essential life skills.

References

Cochrane (2015) *Teaching children in schools about sexual abuse may help them report abuse*. Available at: www.cochrane.org/news/teaching-children-schools-about-sexual-abuse-may-help-them-report-abuse

Department for Education (DfE) (2015) *Personal, social, health and economic (PSHE) education: A review of impact and effective practice*. Available at: https://fs.hubspotusercontent00.net/hubfs/20248256/Vision/PSHE%20a%20review%20of%20impact%20and%20effective%20practice.pdf

Equality Act 2010, c. 10. Available at: www.legislation.gov.uk/ukpga/2010/15/contents

Goldfarb, E. S. and Lieberman, L. D. (2021) Three decades of research: The case for comprehensive sex education. *Journal of Adolescent Health*, 68, (1), 13–27.

Gray, C. (2015) *Carol Gray: Social Stories™*. Available at: https://carolgraysocialstories.com

Renold, E. et al (2023) *"We have to educate ourselves": how young people are learning about relationships, sex and sexuality*. Available at: https://learning.nspcc.org.uk/media/3138/sexuality-education-plus.pdf.

Sex Education Forum (2022) *Relationships and sex education: The evidence*. Available at: www.sexeducationforum.org.uk/sites/default/files/field/attachment/RSE%20The%20Evidence%20-%20SEF%202022.pdf

UNESCO (2009) *International technical guidance on sexuality education: An evidence-informed approach for schools, teachers and health educators*. Available at: https://unesdoc.unesco.org/ark:/48223/pf0000183281